What people are saying abo...

GODSPEED

"Britt Merrick writes like a man who is empowered by the Spirit, is in love with Jesus, and fully trusts the Scriptures. I prayed consistently as I read this book that God would give us more men of this conviction, passion, and seriousness all wrapped up in the joy that only comes in seeing Jesus as the glorious, good God He is. Read this book and buy a few copies to give away to friends!"

Matt Chandler, lead pastor of The Village Church, Dallas, Texas, president of Acts 29 Church Planting Network, and author of *The Explicit Gospel*

"'Godspeed' is a blessing we often give before friends embark on a significant journey—and that's exactly what Britt Merrick does in his new book. Sure, there's a little 'jolt' included to get us moving, but *Godspeed* is a road map for the church as we become the people we are destined to be: God's people moving throughout the world for His glory. Britt leads the way with authenticity and the fresh approach of a follower still feeling the wide-eyed wonder of the grace that propels us to carry the hope of Jesus to every person on the planet. Get *Godspeed* and enjoy the ride."

Louie Giglio, pastor of Passion City Church/ Passion Conferences and author of *Indescribable*

"My friend Britt Merrick colorfully and convincingly shows that God is on a mission to make all things new and that Christians have been rescued to become witnesses of this on-the-way newness by engaging our world, not isolating ourselves from it. To be sure, the parks we make will grow over with weeds, and the buildings we erect will rust, decay, and burn. Yet in the brokenness and transience of our efforts, we will give the world a snapshot of the world that is to come in which 'neither moth nor rust destroys and where thieves do not break in and steal' (Matt. 6:20). Thank you, Britt, for reminding us that we're all missionaries and that the best is yet to come."

Tullian Tchividjian, pastor of Coral Ridge Presbyterian Church, Ft. Lauderdale, Florida, and author of *Jesus + Nothing = Everything*

"What an encouraging, convicting, and eminently practical book Britt Merrick has given us. *Godspeed* shows us how living at the speed of the gospel propels us into a Trinitarian way of living and loving. And to think, God has written *us* into this irrepressible story of redemption and restoration. What a privilege, what a joy. Get and read, share and live this book with your friends."

Scotty Smith, founding pastor of Christ Community Church, Franklin, Tennessee

"With passion, clarity, and unwavering truth, Britt Merrick points us back to a mission worth giving our lives to. *Godspeed* will knock you off the dead-end road of religion and unleash a world-changing adventure with God."

Mike Foster, cofounder of People of the Second Chance

"Few people have helped me understand Christ and His mission like Britt Merrick. I pray and trust that this much-needed book will do the same for you."

Tim Chaddick, pastor of Reality Los Angeles

"Britt Merrick is a leader who lives what he speaks. Read this book. It will inspire you to audaciously live what you believe."

Jeff Shinabarger, founder of Plywood People

"This book is a jolt of missional adrenaline! In *Godspeed*, Britt Merrick calls the church to embark on the journey of a lifetime: and it's called 'Missio Christi,' or the mission of Christ. *Godspeed* is so thoroughly encouraging and radically convicting—this is a book you simply must read!"

Mark Batterson, pastor of National Community Church and author of *The Circle Maker*

"My new friend Britt challenges the church to be more than just a place where saints sit, soak, and sour. By giving us practical examples from his life and Reality church, Britt challenges us all to participate in the mission of God for the sake of the world. This is a wake-up call for the American church."

Darrin Patrick, lead pastor of The Journey and author of *For the City* and *Church Planter*

"I'm so thankful for Britt Merrick. You cannot help but have your heart and mind explode with passion for being on the mission of Jesus after reading *Godspeed*—not just a quick-reaction type of passion that will fade but a deep one based out of the heart of Jesus that impacts the core of our being. This book will not only deeply impact those who read it, but it will impact so many more who will be influenced by those who read it. I look forward to hearing the stories of how God will use this book in the lives of so many people."

Dan Kimball, on staff at Vintage Faith Church
and author of *Adventures in Churchland*

"*Godspeed* throws a grenade of truth into a world where it's so easy to think you've got to come up with your own mission in life. Britt offers a beautiful, compelling reminder that we've already got a mission: Christ's mission."

Jon Acuff, *Wall Street Journal* best-selling
author of *Quitter* and *Stuff Christians Like*

"Christians must regain their identity as being sent by God, and after reading *Godspeed*, I am more convinced of this than ever before. Britt does a marvelous job both theologically and practically of helping us reach that end. Don't just read this book—*do this book*!"

Dave Lomas, pastor of Reality San Francisco

"Britt Merrick has written an important, inspiring, and challenging book. And it's a book rooted in deep experience, not just theory. As a church planter, pastor, and movement leader, Britt has given rich insight into how to be not just a faithful, but also a provocative people of God in these uncertain times. Highly recommended."

Jon Tyson, pastor of Trinity Grace Church,
New York, and author of *Rumors of God*

GODSPEED

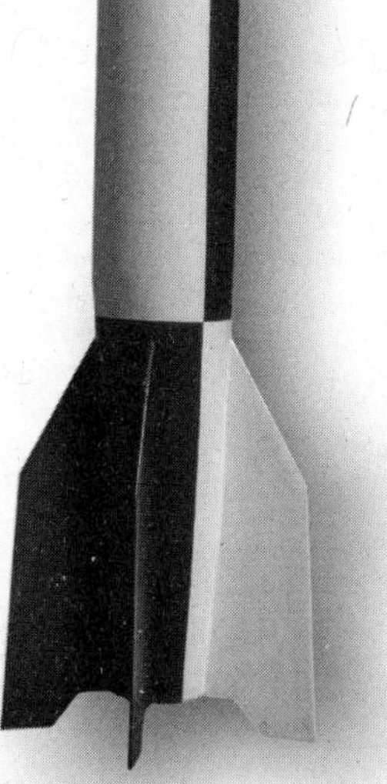

MAKING CHRIST'S MISSION YOUR OWN

BRITT MERRICK
WITH ALLISON TROWBRIDGE

GODSPEED
Published by David C Cook
4050 Lee Vance View
Colorado Springs, CO 80918 U.S.A.

David C Cook Distribution Canada
55 Woodslee Avenue, Paris, Ontario, Canada N3L 3E5

David C Cook U.K., Kingsway Communications
Eastbourne, East Sussex BN23 6NT, England

The graphic circle C logo is a registered trademark of David C Cook.

LCCN 2012930190
ISBN 978-0-7814-0754-0
eISBN 978-1-4347-0501-3

Published in association with literary agent Don Jacobson of D.C. Jacobson & Associates LLC, an Author Management Company www.dcjacobson.com.

The Team: Alex Field, Amy Konyndyk, Jack Campbell, Karen Athen
Cover Design: Nick Lee
Cover Photo: Shutterstock

Printed in the United States of America
First Edition 2012

1 2 3 4 5 6 7 8 9 10

033012

This book is dedicated to my parents, Al and Terry Merrick, who have been the most enduring example of life on mission I have ever seen. I love you guys. Thank you.

CONTENTS

PREFACE

Something's Missing

As the Father has sent Me, I also send you.

Jesus

Do you ever feel like the American church is missing it?

Maybe most of the time you feel okay. You go to church on Sundays, hang out with Christians on weekdays, and spend your vacation time taking missions trips to third-world countries.

And these all are wonderful things.

But do you ever have those moments? You know, when you read the Gospels and then look at yourself and look at the church, and just wonder: *Are we missing it?*

Today more than 85 percent of non-Christians characterize the American church as antihomosexual, judgmental, and hypocritical.[1] We may look okay to one another, but to those outside church walls, we look very little like the Jesus they've heard about. Somewhere between accepting the gospel for ourselves and delivering the good news to others, we've gotten off course. Somehow we've turned grace into condemnation, relationship into rules, and truth into judgment.

Our Christianity has lost sight of the person of Christ.

When we read the Gospels, it's clear that Jesus was on a mission. He ignored cultural norms to seek the broken, He defied social boundaries to touch the untouchable, and He challenged the nature of justice to free the guilty. Jesus, fully God and fully man, upheld the law perfectly and bore its consequence on the cross to bring salvation for all humanity. He was raised from the dead; conquered sin, death, and the devil; and ushered in a kingdom of victory.

Then in John 20:21, before ascending to glory, Jesus made a single statement that set the course for all of Christianity:

"As the Father has sent Me, I also send you."

Before He left the earth, Jesus called His followers to continue His work. He called them to *Missio Christi*: the mission of Christ to save the world.

What would the church look like today if we actually did this? If our lives were extensions of the mission of Christ on earth, would the statistics be so bad? Would humanity respond to the church in the same way?

This book is about mission. But don't give up yet.

I know you may not be a missionary, and maybe you think that if you become one God will send you to remote and distant jungles to minister to cannibals. If that doesn't sound enticing, you're in luck, because I'm not going to ask you to go somewhere else or to become someone else. This book is about a different type of mission, and it's not what we've been doing in church-as-usual.

The first verse of Acts references "all that Jesus *began* to do and teach." This means that Christ is still doing and still teaching today: *He is presently on mission in our world.* For years the church has said, "Let's go on mission in the name of Jesus." What we should be saying is, "Let's *be* on mission *with* Jesus."

You have been put on earth, in this time and place, where you are right now, for Missio Christi. Our goal, as individuals and as the gathered church, is to figure out what Christ is presently doing and then to do it with Him.

You don't have to make up a mission yourself.

What you *can* do is join in the mission of Jesus that's happening all around you.

Missio Christi is about being who you are where you are, but beginning to live with faithful, missional intentionality.

GODSPEED

I believe that a right understanding of mission is what's missing in the church today.

When we understand our mission, respond to our calling, and live as a people sent by God, we become more like Jesus to the world. Following His example, we'll seek, touch, free, and restore the hurting people all around us. The Holy Spirit will work through us to renew humanity for the glory of Christ and the advancement of His kingdom. We will finally live for something bigger than ourselves—what I call "living at *Godspeed*."

In the pages that follow, we'll look at stories of Jesus and the people He loved: adulterers, demoniacs, social outcasts, and oppressors. We'll look at where the church has gotten it wrong and why, and we'll look at what this means for you and me.

Before we get to the risqué and the radical, we'll lay down a base that's theological in the first few chapters. Stick with me—because theology means something to you. This stuff is also the foundation of our understanding of mission, because a teaching that's not grounded biblically is not a teaching worth living by. I think you'll be surprised by what awaits.

When we actually live like Jesus did, mission gets messy, unpredictable, unconventional—and a whole lot more fun.

If we truly grasp the calling Jesus gave us in John 20:21, it will completely change the way we live out our Christianity.

And that will change the world.

PART 1

THE FATHER'S MANDATE FOR MISSIO CHRISTI

"As the Father ..."

1

MISSION

It's Not about People

There is no participation in Christ without participation in His mission to the world.[1]

International Missionary Council

Not too long ago I had the most amazing experience with Jesus. Not "amazing" in the sense of the latte you had the other day, but *actually* amazing.

Our Reality church team had started a new campus in Santa Barbara, California. We poured months of prayer, labor, and resources into the launch. It was difficult work that faced lots of spiritual warfare, with various struggles and hurdles to overcome. As the months marched toward the launch date, I began to doubt whether or not we were doing the right thing. I thought Christ had called us to this, but the process had been so draining and difficult that it left my mind reeling. *Had I led us wrong? Was this more about my own mission than Christ's mission? Did I lead our church into something that had more to do with my ego than God's glory?*

I was starting to panic inside.

Finally the launch date arrived, and we gathered everyone for our first service at the new campus. After many months of prayer, planning, and hard work, we opened the doors, and the place absolutely packed out. But that didn't mean anything to me; drawing a crowd means very little in the scheme of things. As the service began and I got ready to take the platform to preach, I was still questioning the whole thing in my mind, and honestly, I was afraid.

Then it happened.

I walked on stage, and Jesus was there. Not physically. But in some way that I can't fully describe to you now, Jesus was just there. When I got to the pulpit, He put His arm around me and whispered in my ear, "I've been waiting for you. You are exactly where you are supposed to be. Let's do this together."

And at that moment I knew everything would be okay.

JESUS AND THE GREAT COMMISSION

Somber trepidation filled the room. Men spoke in hushed tones behind the bolted door, fearful of the powerful Jewish leaders who were surely hunting them by now.

Jesus was dead. The emptiness in the air felt oppressive, palpable.

Then suddenly something changed.

A man stood among them.

Audible gasps sounded across the room. Disciples collapsed to the floor as their knees gave way; others staggered back in shock.

"Peace be with you!" Jesus, Immanuel, said with a smile.

Nothing moved; no one could breathe.

Jesus stepped closer to His motionless followers and held out His hands. Wide-eyed, they drew near, and He showed them the wound in His side.

Realization and joy hit at once, and the room erupted into celebration. Jesus was alive! Their Lord and their God stood among them.

"Peace be with you!" Jesus said again. The group buzzed with excitement.

Jesus stepped back and waited for the disciples to calm down. They turned their eyes on Him, and then, with all authority, He said the words that would direct the course of His church from that point forward throughout history: "As the Father has sent Me, I also send you."[2]

LOSING THE *S*

Like many Christians, you've probably been on a missions trip before or at least supported one in some way. If so, you know that everything about a missions trip is intentional: where you go, when you go, those with whom you go, and those to whom you go. A bad missions trip isn't one where something goes wrong—you know, like getting sick, needing to separate amorous youth group members, losing the team's luggage, or having twenty heads infected with lice. It turns out that great ministry and new relationships are often cultivated in the worst of scenarios. A bad missions trip is one where nothing is planned or intentional.

Intentionality is the reason why a missions trip to Fiji is different than a Fijian vacation. It's the reason why your friends and family contribute financial support for the former but (unless you're incredibly lucky) probably won't for the latter. If nothing on a trip is *intentionally* missional, then it's just another trip.

I've come to dislike the term *missions*. Because of the misunderstanding of this word and concept, we've begun believing that "missions" is something done by other Christians "over there." In doing church-as-usual, we've lost the biblical notion that each of us has been sent to the world, on mission, within our immediate contexts.

This book, therefore, is not about "missions."

It's about mission.

It's about the mission of Christ to the world and our specific place within that mandate. *Your place in it.* We're going to drop the *s* permanently. It's time to get on a new trip.

Mission is the single reason why your life's purpose is different from most of the rest of the world. Christians are unique, in part, because of their intentional participation in the mission of Jesus Christ. You are unique because of this call. The American church has believed that if we simply send money to other Christians overseas, then they will fulfill our call to mission for us. We've believed that if we spend a week of the summer performing evangelistic mime skits on the streets of Mexico City, then we can check "missions" off our yearly to-do lists.

The presupposition of this book is that we've had it wrong *all this time.*

A Christian's entire life is the mission trip.

A SENT PEOPLE

In the same way the Father sent the Son, Jesus sends us, the church, on mission. Through the Great Commission, He invites us into a purpose that is bigger than ourselves. We have the opportunity to exist for something greater than our own dramas, our own wants, our own needs, and our own dreams. This fact should blow our minds: that with all our flimsy, fleshly, and cheesy humanity, the Creator would still ask us to share in what is most important to Him.

Being on mission is the paradigm shift of a lifetime. The greatest adventure is to hear the invitation and respond. The greatest tragedy is to ignore our calling and go on living life as usual.

The goal of this book is to see every Christian liberated to live on mission and in motion for the glory of God and to help the church learn to live like Jesus did: with missional intentionality.

Don't miss this! It's the chance of a lifetime—the chance of eternity, actually.

Christ was on a mission: the Father sent Him for the glory of God and for the salvation of humanity. And then Jesus said, "As the Father has sent Me, I also send you."

Don't hear "I also send you" as Jesus saying you need to go somewhere else. Hear it as Jesus telling you that you have *already* been sent to where you are right now. Like it or not, you are a sent person.

In the same way the Father sent Jesus, He sends us to the world, empowered by the Holy Spirit for His mission. Understanding this mandate for mission is crucial to our ability to live out our calling as Christians.

To live life at Godspeed.

Before we examine what this is and how we do it, let's begin with the Who and the why, the reason and the purpose, behind our mission. I can't think of any better place to start.

THE END GOAL

Mission begins, and ends, with God.

He is the inventor, initiator, owner, author, finisher, and the goal of mission. All ministry is God's ministry, and all mission is God's mission.

Realigning our lives to work alongside Christ begins by forming a theocentric understanding of mission. *Theo* means "God"; therefore, we're talking about a God-centered understanding of what mission looks like. So when we think about life on mission, there is a single foundational element that must always be in place. This foundation requires that we center on the purposes of God, the heart of God, the revelation of God, the gospel of God, and the triune person of God.

Numerous ideologies compete for this centricity, this foundational place in our worldview. How many Christian leaders operate from an ecclesiocentric, or church-centered, understanding of mission? How many Christians push cosmocentric, or world-centered, objectives? Much of mainstream Christian culture follows an anthropocentric, or human-centered, understanding of mission.

Yes, God calls us to relieve suffering and bring about justice—*absolutely*. But God and His glory must be the driving force for this mission, not the plight of humanity.

One of the opening lines from John Piper's famous book *Let the Nations Be Glad!* is "Mission exists because worship doesn't."[3] The goal of all Christian activity is to glorify God; therefore, we are on mission to the places in the world where worship isn't happening.

The goal of all mission is the glory of God, first because God is worthy of all glory and also because humanity is healed in worshipping God. Every evil we see in the world today is rooted in idolatry that stands in disobedience to the first commandment, "You shall have no other gods before Me,"[4] and fails to heed Jesus' greatest command to "love the Lord your God with all your heart, and with all your soul, and with all your mind, and with all your strength."[5]

When we exalt anything or anyone to a functional place in our lives higher than God, the result is destruction and a broken world. But when Christ is in His rightful place upon the throne, humanity is healed.

BLESSED TO BE

To have a biblical understanding of mission is to realize that the Bible is a book about God—*not about us.*

This might come as a shock if you've been reading your Bible through me-colored glasses: *I'm messed up … I need something … I'm broken … I'm dissatisfied. Something is wrong. Where's the answer? What's that verse again?*

In truth, the Bible is the story of God's mission in the world as it unfolds throughout human history.[6] Christianity gets fun when we understand our salvation through the perspective of who God is and what He's doing in the world! The Bible comes alive when we read it missiologically, with a lens that looks for the mission of God.

When we see the grand story of God's mission to redeem, restore, and heal humanity, it's a massive paradigm shift. We realize that life is not about us or what we want to do—and that's a relief, because I'm already sick of myself. Life is about God and His glory and what He is doing. The more we get caught up in that reality, the more we are free to be who God is calling us to be.

The question "What should I do?" becomes "What is God doing?"

When we view Scripture with an eye toward what God has done, is doing, and will do, all questions of "What should I do now?" get answered.

Throughout history God has worked *through* people rather than *independent of* people. This is one thing that the metanarrative of the Bible reveals. One of the first and most profound places we see this truth in Scripture is in Genesis 12. It is the functional beginning of the mission of God in human history, given through the Abrahamic covenant:

> Now the LORD said to Abram, "Go forth from your country, and from your relatives and from your father's house, to the land which I will show you; and I will make you a great nation, and I will bless you, and make your name great; and so you shall be a blessing; and I will bless those who bless you, and the one who curses you I will curse. And in you all the families of the earth will be blessed."[7]

Revealed here is another foundational piece of the bedrock of our involvement in God's mission: *God blesses us to bless others.*

God called Abraham, He sent Abraham, and He blessed Abraham. God chose to bless all nations through Abraham. The process is the same for the Christian: God called us, He sent us, and He blesses us to bless others. Not because we are awesome, but because He is awesome.

The last thing we want to do then, by self-absorption or self-centeredness, is to become a clog in that flow. It is our human and cultural tendency to want God to bless us, just for us. But the truth is that God blesses us so that we will do something with that blessing. *So that we might bless others.* He blessed Abraham and said, "So you shall be a blessing … and in you all the families of the earth will be blessed."[8]

When we understand this truth, we live differently.

The last few years have been the most difficult season of my life. Ironically they have also been the most blessed.

It began one Monday morning when my wife and I got an urgent call from our five-year-old daughter's elementary school. There had been an accident, and she was rushed to the hospital where a CAT scan revealed that her tiny body contained a Wilms' tumor, a rare form of kidney cancer. The tumor was the size of a Nerf football, and it was hemorrhaging cancerous cells into her body. There began our family's long, tumultuous battle with cancer.

In those first weeks our church family flooded us with support. People we didn't know, from all over the world, began sending us gifts and cards and little presents for our daughter, Daisy Love. Today I can safely say she has more stuffed animals than can fit in her room.

Some people, who no doubt are parents, were so savvy and thoughtful that they anticipated what Daisy's eight-year-old brother, Isaiah, might be going through. He watched all this happen to his little sister and witnessed the massive outpouring of attention and gifts heaped on her. Surely he was dealing with fear, insecurity, and jealousy, as any of us would. So every once in a while, he would get a gift in the mail too.

The week I began teaching a series on mission at our church, someone sent my son a gift card for California Pizza Kitchen: *twenty-five bucks*. What a cool thing to send to an eight-year-old! When we explained to him how it worked, his immediate reaction was "Oh! I can take my Auntie Heidi and Uncle Johnny out to lunch with this card. It's her birthday this week!" Isaiah made the plans and got some money for a tip, and that week he took his aunt and uncle out to CPK and spent the entire card on them.

Afterward it hit me: my eight-year-old gets what so few of us in the church understand.

God blessed him to be a blessing.

This simple principle is the foundation of how God works through humanity. The work is God's work and the blessing is God's blessing, but He delivers His blessings through you and me.

THE WHOS AND THE WHAT

We're going to get a little theological here, but bear with me. I promise we'll get into judging others and adultery and demons later on.

Mission is not primarily an activity of the church; rather mission is an attribute of God. Let me explain.

To be a Christian is to be a Trinitarian. It's a weird word that sounds like a galaxy from *Star Wars*. But it explains the mystery of the essence, the intrinsic nature, of God.

We believe that God is one, as it says in Deuteronomy: "*Sh'ma Yis'ra'eil Adonai Eloheinu Adonai echad.*" Or in English, "Hear, O Israel! The LORD is our God, the LORD is one!"[9] God is one, or "*echad*," as it's called in Hebrew. Yet while God is one, He is also three.

Jesus expressly revealed the Trinitarian nature of God in the Gospels. "I and the Father are one,"[10] He said, and commanded His church to baptize "in the name of the Father and the Son and the Holy Spirit."[11] It's one name but three distinct persons. This plurality—Father, Son, and Holy Spirit—exists in a unity of being: three Whos and one What.[12]

Can you wrap your mind around that? I can't. The Trinity is a mystery because our finite minds cannot comprehend the infinite nature of God.

I remember an old G. K. Chesterton quote that went something like "If God were simple enough for me to understand, He wouldn't be great enough to meet my needs nor worthy of my worship." We must beware any concept of God we can fully understand, for that is no god at all.

The triune nature of God is a mystery, but it's not a contradiction. The teaching is made clear throughout Scripture, even though we can't fully understand it. Most Christians will leave Trinitarian doctrine here—*as a mystery*—and move on. But there is more.

In His very nature, God is a missionary God. We begin to comprehend this when we look at the relational life of the Trinity.

Before anything else existed, God was. Father, Son, and Holy Spirit, He has always existed in community. "God is love," we read in 1 John 4:8,[13] and such love must have an object, an action, and an opportunity. It is the very nature of love to be others-centered. The dynamic love of the Godhead flows outward toward humanity, and it broke into time and space at the moment of the incarnation. Mission is the love of God moving for God's glory; Jesus is the love of God manifest in human history. Therefore, because God is love, God is always on mission.

It's a lot of theology, but track with me.

When we are saved, we enter into life with the triune God. We "become partakers of the divine nature," reads 2 Peter 1:4. As Christians, we understand our salvation as "Christ in us"—what Colossians calls "the hope of glory."[14] Meanwhile, the New Testament refers to us as "those who are in Christ,"[15] and in John 17, Jesus prayed that as the Father is in Him and He is in the Father, so we would be in Them.[16]

We are in Christ and Christ is in us. This means we participate in the life of Jesus. Throughout the Bible we see the Father, Son, and Holy Spirit engage with one another. The Trinity is participatory. As Christians, you and I are invited into the life, into the love, and into the reality of the triune God through the cross of Jesus Christ.

If God by nature is a missionary God, then Christians by their new nature, having been remade in the image of God, should live as missionary people.

Are we participating in God's nature?

DON'T "GO" TO CHURCH

The chief evangelistic strategy of many Christians today is to invite nonbelievers to church. But our lives, on the whole, are not witnessing to the effects we claim church to make. Imagine you knew a person who was in terrible health and was always nagging you to eat spinach, like he or she did, for all its physical benefits. You wouldn't buy the argument, because there was no proof in that person's life to support his or her claim.

The church today doesn't have a great reputation. While 84 percent of not-yet Christians in America have a relationship with a Christian, only 15 percent of them say they have observed any significant difference in that Christian's life.[17]

It would be one thing if we were telling people to eat spinach and we looked like Popeye. It's another thing when our lifestyles don't reveal that the "spinach" has done us any good.

Church is not the goal of mission or the gospel. Don't get me wrong, church is great—I'm a pastor, and I love church—but some of us think we get saved and go to church and that's it. But that's not it. Church is not the goal; rather it is God's express instrument for ministry and mission.[18]

I want to take this opportunity to undo some of our disconnected thinking about the church and reconnect it to a biblical viewpoint of mission.

Disconnect: We think our individual salvation and individual worship of God is the goal. *Reconnect:* Although our individual salvation and worship are important, the goal is the renewal of the world and the worship of God by all peoples. When we get saved and become members of the church at-large, it is not the end but the beginning.

Disconnect: We see the church as a place to meet our personal needs—spiritually, relationally, physically, and socially. *Reconnect:* The church does not exist to meet our needs but is a means through which God meets the needs of the world. When we shift our thinking about why the church exists, it radically changes the way we participate in the church.

Disconnect: We see mission, or "missions," as one of the many programs of the church in which we may or may not participate. *Reconnect:* Mission is not a program of the church—*mission defines the church*. It is not one thing we do out of many opportunities. Mission is core to our identity as God's people.

Disconnect: We send people off to other places to do "missions." *Reconnect:* We have been sent to right here, to our own time and place, to do mission. When we only send people overseas or to other places on "missions trips," we perpetuate the misunderstanding that it's an "over there" program. The real opportunity for mission, God's mission, is all around us in our own contexts.

OUR IDENTITY AS THE CHURCH

My church in Santa Barbara, Reality, sends people overseas all the time. We bring them forward, we lay hands on them, and we pray over them for the anointing and empowering of the Holy Spirit. That's biblical—it's what the church did for Paul and Barnabas in Acts 13. This practice in itself is right, but we've messed it up. As American Christians, we now sit in the pews and think, *They are sent. They do our mission. Mission happens in other places. What's for lunch?*

But God sent us all to the world to live on mission within our own surroundings. At Reality, we of course won't stop laying hands on people when they go to foreign countries, but we need to do more. Maybe we need to start holding sending ceremonies for those of us who are staying put! Praying over the teachers and the plumbers and the students and the business people who live on mission in their backyards, at their jobs, schools, and communities.

The church is the people of God called to God sent by God for the glory of God to meet the needs of the world *with God.*

That is our identity.

There are two driving factors of this identity that we must keep in mind at all times: The first driving factor is the glory of God. Mission is propelled by a deep love for and the worship of the name of God.[19] "The love of Christ controls me," Paul wrote in 2 Corinthians 5:14. The ultimate purpose of mission is to bring God glory—to encourage His worship, His praise, and His adoration among all peoples.

The second driving factor is our identity in Christ. As the people of God, all mission flows from our Jesus-given identity: saved, reconciled, adopted, beloved. Jesus saved us, so we seek to see others similarly redeemed. Jesus reconciled us with God, so we work to see others restored to God and to one another. Jesus adopted us, so we care for other people who might also be adopted by God. And finally, God loves us, so we love others with the same love that Christ has poured out onto us.

Everything we do flows out of our identity as God's sent people, and all Christian activity drives toward the glory of God.

If we understand ourselves as a sent people, then we are not called to *go* to church. We are called to *be* the church. If all professed Christians truly lived as the church, the result would shake the world.

INTO THE MISSION FIELD

The Modern Missionary Movement began in 1792 and continues into this present day.[20] It has been the most successful period of mission in the history of the church.

The movement reportedly began with William Carey, a shoemaker from England. Carey was a self-educated young man with a heart after God. By the time he was twenty-one, he had mastered Hebrew, Greek, Latin, and Italian. (I know, what have we been doing?)

One day young William fashioned himself a globe out of shoe leather and began reading the diaries of Captain Cook. What he gleaned from these geographical accounts was the immense need for Christ around the world. He developed a burden for the nations and a heart for the mission of God and the ministry of the gospel.

In 1792, Carey wrote a book called *An Enquiry into the Obligations of Christians to Use Means for the Conversion of the Heathens in Which the Religious State of the Different Nations of the World, the Success of Former Undertakings, and the Practicability of Further Undertakings Are Considered.*

The book you're reading is called *Godspeed*—and apparently its title needs about forty more words.

In the same year Carey wrote the book with that overlong title, he preached a sermon titled "Expect Great Things from God; Attempt Great Things for God" that changed the world. Men and women began a movement toward the nations.

Two years later Carey went to India. He served the Lord there for forty-three years and saw incredible fruit.

All of the movement's controversy and human failings aside, we can confidently say that this period of missionary work has been remarkably successful for worldwide evangelization.

For many years the church in North America has sent missionaries to the nations. Yet in recent years the American church has suffered a loss not only in church membership but also of influence.[21] We've lost influence for the gospel and influence for Christ within our own society.

How then should we view North America?

Are we to see ourselves as an evangelized people or as a mission field?

In 1908, Pope Pius X terminated the mission status of the American church.[22] Whether that was right or wrong for the Catholic Church to do in 1908, I can't say. I wasn't there. But when I look around North America today, I see a culture that is far from Christ, a society in rebellion against God. I see a church that has lost focus on Jesus. I see a perverted gospel and an increasingly anti-church, anti-Christian, anti-Christ spirit at work all around.

If North America was ever evangelized, it no longer is today.

We live in a post-Christian society that is rapidly becoming anti-Christian. Why this concerns me is not because the church needs political influence or because I'm afraid of being marginalized. Historically the church has worked best from the margins. This bothers me because I want every person to know and enjoy Jesus, and I don't want men and women to go to hell.

So I believe it is fair and proper to speak of North America as a full-blown mission field. If you don't agree with me, please think about your workplace, your school, your friends, and your family.

Is it a mission field? Do you know anyone who needs Jesus?

Now think about how you came to put your faith in Christ. Did it happen because of a speaker at a festival? Did it occur during a teaching at a major church event? This is the story of some Christians. But for most of us, we accepted Christ as our Savior because we had an authentic relationship with a believer. We knew someone who showed us Jesus.

According to recent statistics, because of America's population of unbelieving people, the nation is now the third-largest mission field in the world.[23]

If we agree that our context is as desperate for Jesus as anywhere else, then how can we be faithful to Him, the gospel, the Scriptures, and our calling here in North America? It's a question we must ask ourselves every day. *How can we be faithful?*

Being sent as Jesus was sent begins with a paradigm shift for the church. A move from thinking that missions is "over there" to realizing that mission is right here. A move from believing missions is something "they" do to realizing mission is what we do. A move from thinking our churches "send" people to realizing that we, as the church, are a sent people.

THAT'S WHAT IT'S ALL ABOUT

The Bible reveals the mission of God unfolding across the centuries and reaching its revelatory climax in the coming of Christ.[24] The ultimate manifestation of God's mission, God's purpose, and God's plan is the person of Jesus Christ.

God's mission reaches its functional climax in Christ's ministry, death, and resurrection. Therefore, all mission centers on the work of Jesus and adheres to the gospel. And God's mission continues through the church. The book of Acts opens by referencing, "All that Jesus began to do and teach ..."

Those two verbs in the Greek, *do* and *teach*, are in the imperfect tense, which means they are ongoing actions. In other words, the mission of Christ never ended. Today Jesus is still doing and still teaching, and He is doing it through His people.

This mission is heading toward a consummation, and the end is not the destruction of all things. The end is the renewal of all things.

Revelation 21:1–5 reads:

> Then I saw a new heaven and a new earth; for the first heaven and the first earth passed away, and there is no longer any sea. And I saw the holy city,

> new Jerusalem, coming down out of heaven from God, made ready as a bride adorned for her husband. And I heard a loud voice from the throne, saying, "Behold, the tabernacle of God is among men, and He will dwell among them, and they shall be His people, and God Himself will be among them, and He will wipe away every tear from their eyes; and there will no longer be any death; there will no longer be any mourning, or crying, or pain; the first things have passed away." And He who sits on the throne said, "Behold, I am making all things new."

There is a finish, a consummation, and a goal. It is the renewal of all things through the person and the cross of Jesus Christ, and He is working that renewal through us today.

God's mission calls us to Himself in worship then sends us out into the world in His service to represent His kingdom and proclaim His gospel, wherever we are.

As the church, we cannot hide: we have an agenda. We don't want people to go to hell, and we want to see them experience the joy of knowing Jesus. We want to see slavery end, people healed, relationships reconciled, marriages renewed, and children loved. Christ's mission continues.

And we are a part of it.

2

CALL

Good News for Us ... In Spite of Us

If God has fit you to be a missionary, I would not have you shrivel down to be a king.

Charles Spurgeon

When my wife and I first sensed the call of God on our lives, it wasn't an extraordinary circumstance. Kate and I were at a surf contest in Southern California. At the time I made surfboards for a living, surfed in contests, and coached teens to do the same.

It was a typical Saturday. Between surf heats, Kate and I had a little down time, so we opened the Bible and began to read.

To tell you the truth, this day was one of the first times my wife and I had read the Bible out loud in public together. If you've ever done this, you know what an experience it can be. Try pulling the Bible out on an airplane sometime: bring one of those huge ten pounders, lay it down, *wham!* on your tray, and start flipping through the pages. Whenever I do this, people look at me like it's contraband. As if they're thinking, *How did he get that through security?*

As Kate and I sat in the sand with our Bible, one of the teens I coached strolled up to us. "What are you guys reading?" he asked.

"The Bible," we answered.

"What's in the Bible?"

"What do you mean, 'What's in the Bible?'" I said. I was naive enough at the time to believe that every American knew what was in the Bible.

"I've never seen one," said the teen.

"Okay …," we began, "Genesis 1 …"

Kate and I literally started at the beginning of the Old Testament and spent the entire day telling this young man about the plan, the heart, the work, and the character of God. That evening we drove the three hours back to Carpinteria together, and before we dropped him off at his house, we finished by telling him about Revelation and the new heaven and the new earth.

Not long after, that young man gave his life to Christ.

In a very normal situation—hanging out on the beach and answering a simple question—my wife and I sensed the call of God upon our lives. Of course we would backslide, we would falter, we would doubt, and I would go on to be the proverbial Jonah. But after that day, after we felt God's call, our lives were never the same.

JESUS AND THE DISCIPLES

Jesus had just begun His public ministry in Israel.

As He traveled along the Sea of Galilee, He saw two fishermen, Simon (later to be called Peter) and his brother Andrew, casting a net into the sea. "Follow Me," Jesus called, "and I will make you become fishers of men."

Immediately the men left their nets and followed Him.

The small group continued walking along the sea. They saw two more brothers, James and John, preparing their nets in a boat with their father, Zebedee. Immediately Jesus called out to them.

And leaving their boat, their father, and all the hired men, James and John came forward to follow Jesus.[1]

NOT MERELY BELIEVING

The first thing Jesus proclaimed at the outset of His public ministry was the coming of the kingdom of God. Next, He gave an invitation to participate in the work of that kingdom.

Early in Mark 1, Jesus came into Galilee, preaching, "The time is fulfilled, and the kingdom of God is at hand; repent and believe in the gospel."[2] He declared that the kingdom had come, and then He offered the disciples an invitation to participate in the kingdom itself.

Looking at the gospel accounts carefully, we can see Jesus leading the disciples into two distinct phases of discipleship. Prior to leaving their boats to follow Jesus in Mark 1, the disciples believed in Him and got to know Him.[3] In the book of John, the men spent time with Jesus. They went with Him to the wedding at Cana,[4] they spent Passover with Him in Jerusalem,[5] and they traveled with Him to witness John the Baptist's ministry.[6] The first phase of discipleship we see is simply believing the gospel and *being with* Jesus.

The second phase of discipleship is participation. This phase goes beyond mere belief; it requires actively going on mission. More than just *being with* Jesus, it's *going with* Jesus. When Jesus called the fishermen, and they left their boats to follow Him, their discipleship entered into its second phase.

Often we refer to this activity as a person's "call" or "calling." We speak of God's calling on a particular person's life or the specific work or mission to which he or she has been called.

The truth is that Jesus calls every Christian.

Most of us speak about this calling in broad terms. God calls us to be ministers of reconciliation, ambassadors for Christ, proclaimers of the gospel, demonstrators of the life of Jesus, and stewards of God's grace.

We know our calling in a macro-sense.

What then is our calling in specific terms? In the minutiae of our lives, in what we do and who we are, in our relationships and in how we spend our time, what is our specific calling?

Every Christian is called. This means every one of us is either fulfilling his or her call or failing in it. Each of us should be able to say, "In my context, this is who Christ made me to be," or in how we spend our time, "This is what I am doing with Christ."

Can you identify your specific calling in Christ?

Do you have any idea what it is?

Unfortunately for the church and for the world today, too many Christians would answer that question with a no.

UPSIDE DOWN AND NORMAL

Peter, a disciple called by Christ, understood the meaning of calling. "You are a chosen race," he wrote to the church in his first epistle, "a royal priesthood, a holy nation, a people for God's own possession, *so that you* may proclaim the excellencies of Him who has called you out of darkness into His marvelous light."[7]

Peter, as one who experienced the call of Christ, said that we are chosen and called in order that we might proclaim and make known the praises of God. Peter described you and me as "a chosen race." This is part of our identity as Christians.

In the previous chapter we defined the church as the people of God, who are called to God and sent by God for the glory of God to meet the needs of the world with God. This is our biblical identity as the church. We are those who work together with God in His mission.[8]

Throughout the Bible we see that God always handpicks His partners: He chose Noah, He chose Abraham, He chose Moses, He chose David, He chose the prophets, He chose the nation of Israel, He chose the disciples, and He chose you and me.

When we look at Scripture—*and when we look in the mirror*—we realize that the people God chooses are *far* from perfect. Noah had a drinking problem that led to some strange situations in his life. Abraham, the father of faith, struggled tremendously with doubt and disbelief that the Lord would actually deliver on His promises. Moses had a multitude of deficiencies: he couldn't speak well, he overreacted, and he disobeyed. David, the beloved king of Israel, was an adulterer and a murderer.

The prophets were no better. Elijah appeared to be suicidal, Jeremiah was depressed, Jonah ran from the call of God, and Isaiah preached naked (honestly, it's in the Bible!). Look at the nation of Israel and you'll see, over and over again in Scripture, that they were a stiff-necked and obstinate people. God refers to them as such.[9]

Therefore, when God calls us "chosen," it ought to yield in us a great humility because of the type of people God chooses. The New Testament says explicitly what the Old Testament illustrates wonderfully:

> For consider your calling, brethren, that there were not many wise according to the flesh, not many

> mighty, not many noble; but God has chosen the foolish things of the world to shame the wise, and God has chosen the weak things of the world to shame the things which are strong, and the base things of the world and the despised God has chosen, the things that are not, so that He may nullify the things that are, so that no man may boast before God.[10]

As the people of God, chosen by God, called forth into mission with Christ, we must allow the Holy Spirit to work a deep humility into us. This begins with the simple understanding that God chooses, as it says in 1 Corinthians, the foolish things of the world.[11]

We learn something about the nature of the kingdom by looking at those whom Christ called. The kingdom of God does not conform to conventional standards of importance, power, and influence—in effect, it's an upside-down kingdom. Jesus announced the coming of a kingdom that will right every wrong and undo evil, but He didn't choose the politically powerful or recruit the influential to join. Jesus didn't go to the elite of Jerusalem; instead He went to a handful of socially insignificant guys in an unnoticed corner of Galilee.

Jesus chose men for His disciples who were as normal as you could find in first-century Jerusalem. The disciples were flawed, proud, self-seeking, weak, shortsighted, and inhospitable men.

When Jesus taught and the crowd got hungry, the disciples' solution was to send them away.[12] When some little children were presented before Jesus for blessing, the disciples rebuked the people who brought them.[13] When a messenger of Jesus was barred from entering a Samaritan village, the disciples asked if they could call down fire to destroy the villagers.[14] And while Jesus agonized in prayer before His crucifixion in the garden of Gethsemane, the disciples fell asleep.[15]

Jesus did not choose followers who were already great people. He chose raw material that He could reshape for a great purpose.[16] Jesus' call to Peter, Andrew, James, and John wasn't "Follow Me because you are ..." His call was "Follow Me, and I will make you become ..." Jesus would take the only trade and context these men knew and make them fishers of men.

Much of the Gospels focuses on the training of the Twelve. Jesus invited them into His mission, and then He initiated a holy process in their lives. The disciples failed and disappointed Him often; however, they were indispensable to Him. Jesus used the disciples as His instruments for mission and as agents through which His kingdom would go forth.

The disciples were raw material, just as you and I are raw material. God chose us, and we are also indispensable to His mission. Imperfect people are vital to the mission of Christ, not because of any deficiency in God but because God's perfect choices aren't based upon worldly criteria.

Christ's sole criterion is His love.

ALL THE RADICALS

God doesn't always call the powerful, but the call itself is always powerful. When Jesus said, "Follow Me,"[17] the English translation doesn't do justice to the written Greek. In the original language, "Follow

Me" is actually a three-word phrase amounting to these words: "Come here behind!"

The phrase is much stronger than "Hey guys, follow the leader." Jesus wanted the disciples with Him, close to Him, following directly behind. It reminds me of how we parents often command our kids to behave when they wander around a busy store: "Come here, behind me." It's the phrase we use to get our children's full attention, obedience, and nearness. Jesus wants the same from His followers.

He called the disciples into a relationship, and what's clear throughout the Gospels is that following Jesus was a relationship of apprenticeship. The disciples became apprentices of Jesus so that they might imitate His life. The New Testament echoes this call to you and me, saying we are to be imitators of God, conformed to the image of Christ.[18]

Jesus' apprenticeship of the Twelve is often compared to that of Jewish rabbis of the day, who commonly had disciples as well. But there's a significant difference between Jesus and your average Jewish rabbi. A rabbi did not call or choose his followers; rather the student adopted the teacher.

However, Jesus chose His twelve disciples.[19] "You did not choose Me but I chose you," Jesus said in John 15, "and appointed you that you would go and bear fruit."[20] Jesus was intentional in this choice, which elicited responsibility from His chosen.

Look at the purposes for which Christ called you: He can use your life, your gifts, your talents, your occupation, your likes, and your preferences, even your flaws—the person He made you to be—to bear fruit for His kingdom.

God has *chosen you* to bear fruit for *His glory* in this world.

The call of Christ is radical, and it requires a radical response. We see this with the fishermen-to-be-disciples in Mark 1. Immediately the men left everything to follow Jesus, and their lives were never the same. These guys faltered and failed, but their participation in Missio Christi changed the course of history.

In understanding the call of Christ, I look around and ask myself, *Where are all the radicals?*

Where are the men and women who will forsake everything to go to the nations? Where are the men and women who will give themselves up to reach those who need Christ most, even those in their own backyards? Where are the men and women who will put affluence and comfort upon the altar and instead choose to change the world with Jesus? Where are those people who will volunteer to die on a sword, hang upside down on a cross, or undergo persecution, beatings, and mocking? Where are those who will pour out their lives like a drink offering in order that others will be saved?

The call of Christ is *radical.* Our response to Christ should be equally radical. Where are the radicals in the American church?

SLEEPING BAGS

The call of Christ is indeed radical, but the occasion of the call itself is often surprisingly normal. Fishermen Peter and Andrew were casting a net, a mundane activity they'd done thousands of times before. James and John were preparing to fish in a boat with their father, a scene as typical as any other day in their lives.

Then, all in an instant, Jesus stepped into their worlds. The God of the universe showed up and invited them to make their lives entirely about His business.

Your call will look different than the call of these disciples. Jesus called them to leave behind their careers to follow Him, whereas Jesus may call some of us to stay right where we are, while remaining faithful. The call of God won't always mean leaving everything. Often it will require us to be faithful in the little things and to follow Jesus' lead from there.

In most cases, the call of Christ comes in everyday circumstances.

When my wife and I first felt the call of God on our lives that day at the beach, we had no idea He would lead us into full-time ministry and eventually to the birthing of churches. I thought I would be shaping surfboards and running a surfboard empire, not shaping hearts with the gospel and shepherding the people of God's kingdom.

For a long time I continued in the former, our family business, while beginning to minister, teach, and disciple. Eventually God led me to a fork in the road. I walked away from the money and the notoriety and my life's passion in order to wholeheartedly pursue the ministry to which God called me. But long before that day, I first heard the call to Missio Christi in the midst of my day-to-day life.

Similarly Jesus found His disciples as they worked, in the midst of their daily routines, and offered them the opportunity to live for something greater—*the eternal salvation of the world.*

God is already at work around us, and He's calling. All we need are ears to hear Him and the obedience and faith to respond.

The week I shared this message with our congregation at Reality, I spoke to a man named Marty from our campus in Ventura. It was wintertime, and Marty had just returned from a dirt-biking, camping trip in the mountains.

The weather was viciously cold, so someone had offered to bring an RV for everyone to sleep in. Unfortunately for the group, they arrived in the mountains to find that whoever was supposed to bring the RV had flaked out or forgotten. So that night Marty and his buddies threw their sleeping bags on the ground and slept outside under the stars.

They froze.

As Marty lay there that night, sleepless and shivering, God spoke to him. He said, *Marty, people who I love sleep this way—but with less—every night in your city.* Jesus put a burden on Marty's heart for the things that burden God's heart.

A week later Marty still couldn't shake the experience. He sent me a text in the middle of the night that read, "We need sleeping bags. We need hundreds of sleeping bags."

I think my initial reaction was something along the lines of *Why did I tell the church I keep my phone by my bed at night?* But by morning my simple charge to Marty was "Do it. Go be the church."

And Marty did it.

That week he organized a sleeping-bag drive across the entire city of Ventura. His garage became the storehouse for more sleeping bags, jackets, and supplies than he could have even prayed for. "God's storehouse," he called it, and spent the next sleepless nights driving around the city in a borrowed van to deliver everything.

Marty isn't normal anymore. He has this passion and drive, because he heard the call of Jesus in a very normal circumstance and responded.

Since that night, God has surrounded Marty with men in the church who share his vision. Their nights on the streets are a battlefield, but wrought with supernatural power and opportunities to love and share the gospel with people who have become "like family." They take calls in the middle of the night and store shopping carts in the garage when someone's put in jail.

"My closeness and intimacy with God has never been like this before," Marty says. "And it has had a beautiful effect on my wife and kids. We began living in a whole new 'outside of the box' way. We call it kingdom living." His dream is to someday find a plot of land he can use for a campground and shelter.

Marty simply got cold one night while camping with friends, and he had ears to hear what the Spirit said. He didn't have to change vocation or location; rather, he just had to be faithful with what he knew was needed right where he was.

MID-CALLING CRISIS

When Christ calls you to join His mission, the calling creates a crisis. It was a crisis for the disciples when they decided to leave everything and follow Jesus. It was a crisis for my wife and me when we shared the gospel with a teen and knew God was calling us to proclaim His Word to others. And it was a crisis in Marty's life too.

The decision to follow the call of Christ is a crisis because it is *costly*. The currency of God's kingdom is servanthood and sacrifice, which require us to give up something, *perhaps everything*. Jesus said that if we're going to follow Him, we better count the cost.[21]

When we sense the calling of God on our lives, it creates a fork in the road. A decision must be made. We will either respond like the disciples did and follow Jesus, or we'll turn away and maintain normalcy.

Peter, Andrew, James, and John left everything to follow Jesus. They left their nets, boats, communities, and lives. James and John left their father, whom they loved and were in business with.

The parting was painful.

If something doesn't hurt, it isn't costly. In Mark 10, when Jesus confronted a rich man who wasn't willing to leave his possessions to follow Him, Peter said, "Jesus, we have left *everything* and followed You."[22] We can almost hear the frustration in his voice. Peter struggled with Jesus' call, and in Luke 5, we see him back in the boat. Peter went fishing, caught nothing all night, and then Jesus again stepped into his world.

The crowds pushed in close to hear Jesus teach, so He climbed into Peter's boat and asked His disciple to put out from the shore. As Jesus spoke to the crowd, all He needed from Peter was for him to hold the boat steady. With complete intentionality, Jesus taught from the vehicle of His follower's livelihood.

Then Jesus flipped Peter's world upside down.

Peter had been out all night on the boat, and he returned without a single fish to show for it.[23] When He finished teaching, Jesus turned to Peter and said, "Why don't you let the nets down for a catch?" Surely Peter was exhausted, frustrated, and defeated by the night's fruitless efforts. The crowd watched as Jesus casually suggested he try once more.

Despite his doubt—and because of who Peter believed Jesus to be—the reluctant disciple let down his nets.

And he pulled up the catch of a lifetime.

When the nets snapped and broke because of the massive amount of fish, Peter called to his companions for help. They filled a second boat with the enormous catch, and both boats began to sink under the weight.

Jesus, of course, didn't perform this miracle for the fish, nor did He do it for the crowd of astonished onlookers. Jesus did it to demonstrate His mastery over that which concerned Peter most.

Peter was following Jesus, but he had returned to fishing. The disciple tried to depend on his own ability. Jesus stepped into Peter's world to display His sovereignty and power.

"Go away from me, Lord!" Peter cried in astonishment. "For I am a sinful man."

But once again, Jesus gave Peter the opportunity to live for something greater. "Do not be afraid," Jesus said, "for from now on, you will fish for people."

In a single moment Peter saw the futility of his values, ambitions, and priorities.[24] And how did he respond?

Peter left the boats and the catch behind and followed Jesus on mission.[25]

FREEDOM

Jesus always pushes His followers to see the value of people through His eyes. Religious leaders often got upset with Him for hanging out with seedy people—*with sinners.* Rather than argue, Jesus spoke to them about things that everyone considered valuable.

"There was a shepherd who lost one of his sheep," Jesus said. "Like any good shepherd, he went after that one sheep, and when he found it, he rejoiced."

"Yes, of course," the Pharisees agreed. "Sheep. That's a valuable thing."

Jesus continued, "There was a woman who lost one of her ten silver coins. She looked all over for the coin, and when she found it, she called everyone to rejoice with her, 'I found my coin!'"

"Yes, of course," they agreed. "A silver coin is valuable."

After getting the Pharisees to agree on the value of things, Jesus then said, "And there was a father who lost a son, and when the son came home, the father rejoiced."[26]

Jesus always established common points of value in order to show the value of people. When religious leaders grew angry with Him for healing on the Sabbath in Luke 14, Jesus said, "Which one of you, if you had a donkey or an ox and it fell into a ditch on the Sabbath day, would not immediately pull it out?"

Of course they all agreed. Then Jesus responded, "So how much more a person?"

Throughout the Gospels, Jesus consistently reoriented perceptions toward the value and priority of people.

When our church began studying the mission of Christ, we created a website called MissioChristi.net where we could talk about theology as a community and share stories of what God was doing. Someone from our congregation posted this story on the site:

> On Monday it was cold and wet and our friends in the streets felt it. One of them died from it. His name was Freedom. Freedom was a paraplegic and a Vietnam vet. I met Freedom on Veteran's Day. And when I met him he was crying for all the boys

> who had died and continue to die in the wars of our nation. Then he told me about his life, how his wife and his children had died and how much he missed them. And then he praised God for His goodness and His love. I was at a complete loss as to what to do with this man, with his life, the tragedy and the pain of it, and yet his joy and perspective on it. And on Monday he died because it was cold and wet and he had no shelter. And I have to confess that I used to think that because we live in sunny Southern California that homeless people wouldn't die from the elements. I was wrong. Freedom was the twenty-eighth person to die on the streets of Santa Barbara this year.[27]

The gospel of Matthew says that when Jesus saw the crowds He had compassion on them because they were harassed and helpless, like sheep without a shepherd. Then He turned to His disciples and said, "The harvest is plentiful, but the workers are few."[28]

The call of Christ is a call to care for people: that we would see people saved for His glory and that we would bring measures of mercy into their misery.

The call of Christ will make us fishers of women and men.

CALLED AWAY

What is the call of Christ upon your life?

Sometimes we can't answer that question until we've answered a different one: What is Christ calling you to leave behind?

It might not be the nets or the boats, but often when Christ is calling us to something, He's simultaneously calling us away from something else.

In order to live at Godspeed, the disciples abandoned everything hindering them from living on mission with Christ. What is Christ calling you to forsake? What is hindering His mission from going forward through your life?

It's a mistake to think your calling is going to look just like Peter's, because the call of every person is distinct. For most of us, Jesus isn't calling us to leave.

Instead He's calling us to stay and be faithful.

Even still, faithfulness often requires us to leave something behind. Whether it's relinquishing a sin, a relationship, a consuming passion, or a selfish comfort, Jesus' call will radically affect our lives.

We the church are a sent people. You and I are called by God to be on mission with Jesus within our current contexts. Going on mission doesn't mean buying a plane ticket. It means going where Christ has already sent us and being faithful to Him there.

Stop reading for a moment, and look around.

Your mission assignment is to this time, to this place, and to the people you interact with along the way.

The call of Christ is always radical, and it is always relational too.

In Mark 1, Jesus called the disciples in pairs. Later in the Gospels, He sent them on mission *as a group*. The mission of Christ always goes forth in community. When we do mission with Jesus, we do mission together with His followers.

The call of Christ is first a call *to* Christ. Our primary pursuit is intimacy with Him, and thereafter we are sent into the world to do His work.

Mark 3 says that Jesus appointed those whom He wanted to be with.[29] Jesus called the disciples to spend time with Him, and then He sent them out to preach the gospel, giving them authority to cast out demons. Here's the key: the disciples went out to do ministry only *after* they experienced intimacy with Christ. They needed to go through phase one of discipleship—knowing Jesus, believing Jesus, and loving Jesus—first. Only then would they enter phase two: going on mission *with* Jesus.

Ministry flows from intimacy. Mission comes from relationship. Whatever Christ calls you to forsake will also be relational in its implications.

What is standing between you and Jesus?

CALLED TO

Take a look at Matthew 28:18–20, or what we historically call the Great Commission:

> And Jesus came up and spoke to them, saying, "All authority has been given to Me in heaven and on earth. Go therefore and make disciples of all the nations, baptizing them in the name of the Father and the Son and of the Holy Spirit, teaching them to observe all that I commanded you; and lo, I am with you always. Even to the end of the age."

The Great Commission is *not* a "Great Suggestion." Before ascending to heaven, the call Christ gave to His global church wasn't a recommendation; it was a commission.

To be commissioned is to be given authority to act on behalf of another. Jesus said, "All authority has been given to Me," and then He told His followers to go in His authority. Jesus authorized us to act in the world on His behalf, according to His nature, baptizing people in the name, the nature, and the identity of the Father, the Son, and the Holy Spirit.

In a pluralistic culture—a society that recognizes numerous popular claims to spiritual truth—we need to know "by what power, or in what name"[30] we carry out mission. Jesus sends us to baptize in God's triune name.

The Great Commission is a co-mission: *the church doing mission with Christ.*

Recently I had separate conversations with two different people about the very tangible calls of God upon their lives. Both of them felt an overwhelming sense of unworthiness for their calls. I know these people intimately. I've observed their lives and can testify to their relationships with Jesus. They both know Christ in ways that I want to know Christ. As I affirmed their separate calls, their responses were the same: "*But I'm not worthy.*"

When Jesus helped Peter catch a miraculous number of fish, what did Peter do? He said, "Go away from me Lord, for I am a sinful man!"[31]

When Isaiah saw the glory of God in its fullness, how did he respond? "Woe is me … because I am a man of unclean lips."[32]

Those who see Christ most clearly also see people clearly, including themselves. Humility is a prerequisite for fruitfulness in the kingdom of God. Jesus gives grace to the humble and is opposed to the proud.[33]

As followers of Jesus, we are accepted, adopted, chosen, appointed, and anointed by the Holy Spirit for Christ's mission. Jesus is already at work in our communities, in our workplaces, in our families, in our friends, and in our lives. All we need are the eyes to see what He is doing, the ears to hear His call, the faith to forsake the things we must, and the humility to follow His Great Commission faithfully.

In the chapters that follow, we will look at what this means for us practically, and we will challenge traditional "churchianity" as we go along. But before we look at what we're called *to do* and how to do it, I'm going to take the next chapter to expose the thing that Jesus says we're *not* supposed to do. A mandate we've sinfully given ourselves. It's something I struggle with consistently (I'd wager you do too) and a subject Bob Marley sang about for years.

3

SENT

Who's to Judge?

The problem with most Christians today is that they would rather be on the judgment seat than on the witness stand.

Anonymous

The more I read and understand about how Jesus lived, the more I discover something in my own life that haunts me today.

I call it the Great Disparity.

The word *disparity* actually means "great difference," and my term is redundant by design.

It's the great, great difference.

Here's what it is.

Suppose I encounter someone in my community who's never heard of Christianity and I tell her, "I'm a Christian. I follow Jesus." Then imagine that she read through the Gospels to discover what I meant. It's at this point that I realize this person will see almost nothing concrete in my life to connect me directly with Jesus.

This great, great disparity is the gap between who Jesus was in the flesh and who my life reveals Jesus to be.

Sure, there are things I could justify to this person: "Oh, well, I'm a lot like Christ in *this* way." She may eventually draw some skewed conclusions, such as, "Britt doesn't get drunk anymore" or "Britt doesn't do this and that anymore." But if she read the Gospels to find out about Jesus, she wouldn't walk away thinking sobriety was a defining trait.

Instead she would discover that Christ loved people and lived with radical mercy, kindness, and grace. She would see that He touched lepers, healed the lame and the sick, sought the broken, restored the oppressed *and* the oppressors, and set the guilty free.

There is a great, great difference between the defining characteristics of Jesus' life and the defining characteristics of Britt Merrick's life.

I wish I was alone in this … but I don't think I am.

A vast majority of the not-yet Christian world sees Christians as judgmental, and according to national statistics, one of the defining impressions of Christians is that we are insensitive to others.[1]

Judgmental and insensitive—*Jesus was neither.*

There is a great disparity today between who Christ was in the flesh and how He's fleshed out in the daily life of the American church.

As Christians, we know that God sent His only Son to save us. We can recite John 3:16 on demand—it's the foundation of our faith. "For God so loved the world …"

But do we know what John 3:17 says?

> *"For God did not send the Son into the world to judge the world, but that the world might be saved through Him."*

LOOK AT CHRISTIANS

As Father, Son, and Holy Spirit, God is at once Sender, Sent, and Sending. As I've said already, God in His very nature is a missionary God, and therefore His followers cannot participate *in* Christ without being on mission *with* Christ to the world.

It's time for the church to recapture its sense of *sent-ness.*

When a man needed to deliver a message in first-century Hebraic culture, it was common for him to send a hired servant. But if the message was important, if he needed someone to safeguard and protect the message, then he would only send his son—*his firstborn.*[2]

"Long ago God spoke many times and in many ways to our ancestors through the prophets," says Hebrews 1. "And now in these final days, he has spoken to us through his Son."[3]

This time the message was too profound, too important. God sent His only Son to ensure salvation was delivered perfectly. God sent Jesus to reveal Himself and to complete the work of redemption in the world.

Being sent biblically means, first and foremost, that the sent one knows the Sender intimately. Speaking of the Father, Jesus said, "I know Him, because I am from Him, and He sent Me."[4] The church is sent in the same way God sent Jesus; therefore, all ministry and mission flow from our intimacy with God.

To be sent is to give glory and honor to the Sender, live in close relationship with the Sender, do the Sender's work, speak the Sender's words, follow the Sender's example, be accountable to the Sender, and exercise the delegated authority of the Sender.[5]

In the Gospels, Jesus perfectly fulfilled the role of a sent son.

He delivered salvation to humanity and became the model for the church on mission.

"No one has ever seen God," says John 1:18 (NLT). "But the unique One, who is himself God, is near to the Father's heart. He has revealed God to us."

Colossians 1:15 calls Jesus "the image of the invisible God." If you want to know what God is like, look at Christ in the flesh. Jesus perfectly represents God. And so the logic goes: If you want to know what God is like, look at Christ. If you want to know what Christ is like, look at Christians. Right?

That's where things start to break down.

As mentioned previously, the vast majority of young, not-yet Christians today say they personally know at least one committed Christian. That's good news. Yet only a fraction think the lifestyle of those Christ followers is significantly different from everyone else's. That's bad news, because it means we're not revealing Jesus to those around us.[6]

The deficiency is not in the design of God. The deficiency is in the faithfulness (or more accurately, the faithlessness) of the church. We have not been faithful in our sent-ness. We don't look a whole lot like Jesus.

THE FOURTH MISSIONARY

As followers of Christ and members of the church, we are baptized into the fount of God's sending love. His love should then flow through us as we reach out to our friends, families, neighbors, coworkers, and communities.

Jesus interceded with the Father asking that this love would be a reality in our lives, "that the love with which You loved Me may be in them, and I in them."[7] We have been invited to partake in the divine nature of a missionary God. Jesus actually prayed that we would do this!

As we discussed earlier, in the Trinity, God is Sender, Sent, and Sending. The Father is the first missionary, who in love created the world and sent His Son to redeem it. The Son is the second missionary, who redeemed all of humanity and creation through His life, death, resurrection, and exaltation. The Holy Spirit is the third missionary, sent by the Father and the Son to convict the world of sin and restore righteousness before judgment.[8]

But it doesn't stop there, because the Spirit moves through people to create and empower the church. God sends the church into the world on mission.

The church must see itself as the fourth missionary.

This reality gives us a deeper impetus for living life on mission. This call goes beyond obeying a command, beyond serving in the church, and beyond working to meet the needs of humanity. When we recapture our sent-ness, we no longer see ourselves as doing things *for* God; we understand that Christian mission is doing things *with* God.

If we were sent just as Jesus was sent, then we must delve deep into the Gospels to understand how Jesus lived out Missio Christi to accomplish the goal of John 3:17: "For God did not send the Son into the world to judge the world, but that the world might be saved through Him." But also, we need to understand what Jesus was *not* sent to do: the first half of John 3:17.

If God did not send His Son into the world to judge it, then He certainly has not sent us for that purpose either.

Before I teach a message to our church, I diligently study the content myself, for I believe nobody has the right to teach others what he or she has not already personally learned by the Holy Spirit. So I have spent a great deal of time allowing God to work on my heart over the issue of judging, and I confess to you here that I have been *busted*. I should be in a lot of trouble, but God's mercy is beautiful.

I have repented of this sin repeatedly.

You may need to repent as well.

THE MARLEY MANTRA

Popular culture makes fun of Christians for being judgmental and insensitive. Think *Saturday Night Live*'s "Church Lady" or the movie *Saved* (I never actually watched it). We know the Bible calls us to speak the truth in love,[9] but our concern for people's eternal well-being and our efforts to communicate gospel truths appear to be ineffective.

Why?

First of all, not-yet Christians don't understand the mission given to us by Jesus to expose corruption and confront darkness, so our efforts to do these things are often received poorly.

Second, at the end of the day, people just want to do whatever they want. "Don't judge me" is an easy excuse. Bob Marley sang about it in the seventies, borrowing and twisting the words of Jesus Himself ("Judge not"). Since then, every entitled teenager, rebellious thinker, and pot smoker (I used to be one) stands behind that same mantra: "Don't judge me."

But there is one more reason why Christians' efforts to be truth tellers in the world are often ineffective: *we truly are judgmental and insensitive.*

The church falls hard when it comes to judgment, and our failure is a barrier to the mission of Christ.

We could complain about the Christians and not-yet Christians who misuse the Marley mantra, but unfortunately that isn't going to help our cause. If we want to advance our ability to live life at Godspeed, we must take a hard look at ourselves and address the areas in which we're judging others.

You and I are supposed to be salt and light in the world, and we're supposed to be salt and light without judging or condemning anyone. That's a bit of a conundrum for the church. Suppose you tell someone he or she needs to repent and get right with Jesus. Is that judgment or truth telling? Let's sort through the difference.

According to Webster's dictionary, to judge essentially means to form an opinion about something or someone "through careful weighing of evidence and testing of premises."[10] Some might call this discernment.

This is *not* the type of judgment Jesus talks about. Governmental authorities and courts of law need to exercise this sort of judging and discernment and are entrusted by God to do so.[11] The church has to weigh evidence in order to biblically exercise discipline and must constantly judge the biblical consistency of doctrinal teachings.

Hebrews 5:13–14 says the Word of God trains us to discern good from evil, and Philippians 1:10 says we're to approve of things that are excellent. You and I are to discern right from wrong in every area of life—in relationships, decisions, situations, and ideas. As Christians, we need to do this all the time.

When Jesus spoke of judging, He wasn't referring to this kind of discernment. He was talking about condemnation.

And unfortunately this is the kind of judgment the church is known for today.

THE MOST OFFENDED PARTY

Our challenge as Christians on mission is to be truth tellers who confront evil *without* condemning people. It's a fine line to walk. And we walk that line by separating the two: evil and people.

This separation isn't to imply that people aren't evil. We are. But the Christian's battle is against the powers and principalities of wickedness and spiritual darkness.[12] God is radically opposed to evil—more than we will ever comprehend—and yet He radically loves people.

Judgment and condemnation are people issues, and they fly in the face of the second greatest commandment: to love our neighbors as ourselves.

How often do we see like-minded Christians get together to talk trash about other Christians? "They're too Pentecostal" or "They're too conservative." We judge other Christians in the church, and then we get together to disapprove of and condemn the world.

The judgment Jesus talked about flows out into public discourse and across like-minded company, but at its core, it is a deep sin issue of the heart. When we—who have earned rejection but were accepted by God through Christ—refuse to extend the same grace and mercy to others, we essentially believe that we are superior. Inadvertently we are saying, "I deserved my forgiveness. They are worse than me. God can forgive me, but I can't get over what they did."

In such thinking, we exalt ourselves over and above others, and infinitely worse, we exalt ourselves over and above the almighty God.

In any issue related to sin, God is always the most offended party. Every sin is against God, according to Psalm 51. If God can extend grace and mercy as the most offended party but we refuse to do so, then we must value ourselves above God. Such thinking is a radical sin in itself.

To correct this, it is imperative that we saturate our thinking and our relationships with the gospel. We deserve to be treated poorly and punished severely, but we have been loved, treated kindly, and shown mercy. We must let these truths radically permeate our beings until they flow into our relationships with the people around us.

You can always discern those Christians who understand the gospel best, because they act most humbly toward other people in their failures.

When the gospel takes root in our hearts, we should become so humbled by the fact that God loves us and is kind to us that we cannot help but view others with kindness and love. This deep humility toward other people is a sign of understanding the gospel and a mark of maturity in the Christian faith.

CROSSING THE LINE

Sometimes it's difficult to discern when we are being judgmental. As the Lord taught and corrected me in this area, I realized that I know what it feels like to be condemned.

I recall a time recently when someone went out of his way to tell me that he believed my character was lacking, my sermons weren't biblical enough, and I didn't express enough of a loving attitude. So this man had decided to leave our church and wanted to make sure I knew how much he disapproved of me before he left. Ouch! Now he may have been right on at least two of the three charges, but telling me that I fell far short of expectations and then leaving was hurtful. Honestly I felt condemned.

When I think through these kinds of interactions, I begin to see how sometimes I do the same thing to others. If I treat someone in a way that made me feel judged in the past, then I've probably crossed the line into judgment myself.

At one point or another each of us has in some way felt condemned. As people on mission with Christ, we must guard our hearts and our mouths from judging in similar ways.

Now I need to clarify something here: if someone points out a behavior or a belief you hold that clearly contradicts Scripture, that person isn't necessarily judging or condemning you. The person is simply pointing out that you are in error. And you need to repent. We are supposed to do this in each other's lives, and we're supposed to do this in the world.

What causes us to cross the line from truth telling to judgment is, in part, *how* we call out errors in others. The way we communicate matters greatly.

Are we calling out error in a spirit of humility and gentleness, looking first to correct the sin in our own lives?[13] Do we do it with an attitude of genuine love, care, and concern for others, considering their situations and plights? If so, calling out wrongdoing in this way is biblical.

The thing that Jesus forbids is our tendency to criticize and find faults in others.

The practice of criticism and faultfinding is deeply ingrained in us as a culture. To a large degree, the reason we dress the way we do, drive the types of cars we do, and decorate our houses the way we do is so that people will like us. Most of our standards for what we deem socially acceptable are largely based upon the realization that we're judging one another *all the time*. American culture judges everything, and as a result, the American church is obsessed with criticizing and faultfinding.

Jesus forbids it.

BEHAVING BADLY

We cross the line from truth telling to judging when we think less of people—or treat them poorly—because of how they behave or what they believe.

Jesus treats us well and thinks well toward us even while we behave and believe badly. "God Himself is kind to ungrateful and evil men," Jesus said in the gospel of Luke.[14] This characteristic is a core component of the character of God.

Many people's favorite life verse is Jeremiah 29:11 (NIV): "'For I know the plans I have for you,' declares the LORD, 'plans to prosper you and not to harm you, plans to give you hope and a future.'"

Do you know the context for this verse?

Israel had disobeyed and done wrong, and God punished them through exile in Babylon. Israel blew it, and at that moment of historical failure, God said, "For I know the thoughts I have toward you … thoughts of peace, and not of evil, to give you a future and a hope."

This is the good news of the gospel. God does not approve of the sin of the world, but He loves the world and forgives our sins by the blood of His Son.[15] This good news must permeate our beings until it forms our identity and shapes our relationships.

People who don't truly understand this good news harshly judge their fellow sinners. Everything becomes a merit-demerit system: they view themselves and other people according to performance-based religiosity.

Maybe this is you. Perhaps you went to church this week because you thought that was a good performance before God. The way you dress, the way you talk, the things you do, the things you *don't* do—all of it is a pass or fail performance. Nothing you do is based on an experience of grace or God's acceptance of you *in spite of you*, and so you put other people on your merit system too.

If this is you, and you have never truly grasped the grace of the gospel, then perhaps you're not giving enough grace to others.

WET HAIR

My wife, Kate, is five feet three inches tall, and I'm six feet six inches tall. Needless to say, there's a pretty significant height difference between us. Understandably I always ask my wife to wear tall shoes so I don't have to break my back to kiss the beautiful little woman.

"Honey, wear some tall heels," I'll say, "like some ten-inch platforms or something!"

But Kate won't wear high heels of any sort.

"If I wear shoes like that," she protests, "people at the church will think I'm a hoochie."

Something happened in my wife's Christian experience that caused her to believe that if she wears a certain height of high-heeled shoes, people at church would judge her.

The church crosses the line from truth telling to judging and condemning when we attempt to hold people to—and punish people for violating—our own rules and standards.

Those who do not understand the gospel always add regulations to Christian living. In failing to understand the grace that Jesus bought at the cross, they manufacture rules to gauge their faith journeys. "This is how a Christian woman ought to dress" some might say. Then they judge others according to their rules and make themselves the standard of holiness.

This self-righteous and unmerciful condemnation based on human standards and human understanding is precisely what Jesus forbids. When we judge this way, we are guilty of blasphemy, because only God can make those rules.

I recently learned of a Christian Bible college in Southern California where some of the young men complained to the leadership about young women who left their dorm rooms with wet hair.

"When I see them with wet hair, it makes me stumble, because I think of them in the shower," the young men insisted.

How did the leadership respond?

In order to prevent the young men from stumbling, the Christian Bible college instated a rule that young women could not leave their dorm rooms until their hair was dry.

Umm, really? That is an utter failure for Christianity.

Is God's Spirit in us if we cannot deal with wet hair? Have we truly experienced Christ's conquering of sin, death, and the devil?

That Bible college, like so many churches in America today, set up its own set of rules and regulations—separate from the standards of Christ—in order to mitigate the risk of these young men faltering in their faith.

What do such rules communicate to the not-yet-believing world? What kind of invitation are we giving to not-yet Christians?

Come to Jesus and be set free! But you'd better dry your hair first.

When the standards of Christians contradict the biblical standards of Christ, it hurts the church's ability to carry out the mission of Jesus.

Romans 14:10, 12–13 says:

> But you, why do you judge your brother? … For we will all stand before the judgment seat of God.… So then, each one of us will give an account of himself to God. Therefore let us not judge one another anymore, but rather determine this—not to put an obstacle or a stumbling block in a brother's way.

God sent us into the world, and while on mission with Jesus and living life at Godspeed, we must free ourselves from faultfinding, criticizing, condemning, and passing judgment. Rather we must concern ourselves with our own behavior so that we do not create stumbling blocks. Not wet-hair types of stumbling blocks but serious actions that will cause others to doubt the power and identity of Jesus.

WHO DO WE LOVE MORE?

The gospel of salvation gets twisted too often these days. American Christians have a tendency to receive redemption: "I'm saved! I'm not going to hell. Hooray!"

And then they go off and live their lives however they want.

But the gospel has relational implications. It changes the way we deal with those who do wrong in the world, and it changes the way we deal with those who do wrong against us.

Here's the distinction: you and I should condemn *what* is wrong but not *who* is wrong. Jesus exemplified this on the cross. "Father, forgive them," He said of those who crucified Him, "for they do not know what they are doing."[16]

If someone does wrong, most of us want to condemn and judge the person. If someone wrongs us personally, often we want vengeance and justice.

I love the way Miroslav Volf explained the difference between justice and forgiveness: "To be just is to condemn the fault and, because of the fault, to condemn the doer as well. To forgive is to condemn the fault but to spare the doer. That's what the forgiving God does."[17]

Forgiving people instead of judging them is an affront to our sense of vengeance—*absolutely*. But vengeance is God's.[18] What forgiveness shouldn't be is an affront to our sense of justice.

Here's why.

Justice happens for the whole world, for every single person, either at the cross in justification or at the throne in final judgment. Therefore, when someone wrongs us, we have a historic and prophetic reason to release him or her from condemnation.

"Never pay back evil for evil to anyone," says Romans 12. "If possible, so far as it depends on you, be at peace with all men. Never take your own revenge, beloved, but leave room for the wrath of God. For it is written, 'Vengeance is Mine, I will repay,' says the Lord."[19]

Martin Luther, explaining the attitude we ought to have toward those who offend us, said Christians should "grieve more over the sin of their offenders than over the loss or offense to themselves." This is radical relational thinking. "And they do this that they may recall those offenders from their sin rather than avenge the wrongs they themselves have suffered."[20]

The truth is, we love ourselves more than we love other people, and so we fail to properly apply the gospel toward them. We are more concerned about the offense against us than the reality that the other person has offended God. We want vengeance more than we want the offending party to experience grace.

Some people have the opposite problem.

Rather than telling the truth and confronting others about sin, they hide behind a common excuse: *"Gosh, I just love that person so much. I don't want to step on their toes. I don't want to create conflict or make them sad by pointing out their sin."*

If this is you, the reality is not that you love the other person too much. More than likely, you love yourself too much and you prefer to save yourself the trouble.

"The Lord's bond-servant must not be quarrelsome, but be kind to all, able to teach, patient when wronged, with gentleness correcting those who are in opposition," says 2 Timothy 2:24–25. The passage continues, and look what's at stake: "If perhaps God may grant them repentance leading to the knowledge of the truth, and they may come to their senses and escape from the snare of the devil, having been held captive by him to do his will."

Somehow we have to find the balance—confronting evil without condemning people—because when we refuse to confront error, we leave people in the hands of Satan's will. And when we choose only to condemn or seek vengeance, we turn both ourselves *and* the other person over to the devil's working.

We have got to get this gospel-saturated, sin-confronting, judgment-free Christian activity down, because the Bible is clear about what is at stake.

PRESSED-DOWN GENEROSITY

Whether we are condemning people or not confronting people, these failures affect our personal relationships with God.

"To sum up, all of you be harmonious, sympathetic, brotherly, kindhearted, and humble in spirit; not returning evil for evil or insult for insult, but giving a blessing instead," says 1 Peter 3:8–9, "for you were called for the very purpose that you might inherit a blessing."

To some degree, in some way, the blessings we receive from the Lord are affected by how we bless others relationally. Jesus said this in Luke 6:37: "Do not judge, and you will not be judged; and do not condemn, and you will not be condemned; pardon, and you will be pardoned."

This is not some sort of karmic theology, as if good deeds come back to us. Nor is it to say our salvation is in danger if we are judgmental toward others. What this verse is talking about is the breaking of intimacy, blessings, and the fullness of God in our lives when we refuse to extend grace and mercy toward others.

The next verse says, "Give, and it will be given to you. They will pour into your lap a good measure—pressed down, shaken together, and running over."

In ancient culture if you went to buy grain, the seller at the market would pour it into your container and say, "There, that's what you paid for." But someone who was incredibly generous would press the grain down for you and shake it together, filling every nook and cranny and giving you extra until your container flowed over into the outer layer of your tunic.

Don't you love the rare occasion when you go to buy a smoothie and the server does this? When the server shakes it together, presses it down, and generously gives you more? (Hopefully not overflowing into your lap in this case.)

Jesus concluded, "For by your standard of measure it will be measured to you in return." If we are generous in pouring out grace and mercy and forgiveness into other people's lives, God is going to deal with us in the same way.

Christ made this equally explicit when He taught His followers how to pray: "Forgive us our debts, as we also have forgiven our debtors."[21] And again in Matthew 6:14–15: "For if you forgive others for their transgressions, your heavenly Father will also forgive you. But if you do not forgive others, then your Father will not forgive your transgressions."

The American church is judgmental, and we need to repent. Too much is at stake. God prefers to act in mercy, but if we condemn others for their failings, we invite the Lord to deal with us the same way.

How then do we prefer to act? Judging, criticizing, condemning, thinking less of, and making ourselves feel better? Or offering the grace, mercy, forgiveness, and generosity we have received?

TAKING IT ON MISSION

As we discover our call and recapture our sense of sent-ness, we take the first step into mission by asking one simple question: *What is God already doing around me?*

Our God is a missionary God—Sender, Sent, and Sending. He is doing something around us—in our families, in our friends, in our coworkers, in our communities, in our country, and in the nations of the world. God is always at work, and this theology frames our worldviews.

Practically, when we begin to read our Bibles missiologically—from Genesis to Revelation—we start to understand God's mission throughout all of history. When we begin to read life missiologically, we start to ask, "What is God doing?" And with this question we come to understand situations differently. Suddenly we see God moving within our lives and working all around us.

Once we start to experience daily life this way, everything changes.

Christianity gets exciting.

Being on mission is the adventure of a lifetime, and it carries the impact of eternity.

PART 2

THE SON'S MODEL OF MISSIO CHRISTI

"… has sent Me …"

4

INCARNATION

The Sacred and the Soccer Games

The Christian ideal has not been tried and found wanting; it has been found difficult and left untried.

G. K. Chesterton

If Scripture were a mountain range, the incarnation of Christ—His birth, life, work, the cross, and His resurrection—would be the tallest, most glorious peak.

In the supreme revelation of love, God came to humanity. He became *like us*—taking on flesh and blood. God incarnate. The incarnate Christ felt our infirmities, was tempted in all the ways we are tempted, and yet was found without sin that He might die a substitutionary death on our behalf at Calvary.

To incarnate essentially means to embody. When Christ became flesh, He embodied the very presence, nature, power, character, and glory of God. "The Word became flesh, and dwelt among us," says John 1. "No one has seen God at any time; the only begotten God who is in the bosom of the Father, He has explained Him." Jesus Christ explains the love and the person of God to humanity in the context of history.

As we've read in John 20:21, the Father sent the Son, and the Son sends us in the same way.

Being on mission then, we incarnate Christ.

In the previous chapter we looked at what it means for us to be sent into the world: what the church is sent to do … and what the church is *not* sent to do.

So what does it mean that we are sent in the same way Jesus was sent? How are we to understand this? How are we to live it?

The chapters to come will be our playbook for mission, based on the historical life of Jesus that is revealed to the church through the Gospels. We'll begin with the bedrock of our calling—the very model of our mission itself—the incarnation of Jesus.

To live at Godspeed is to do mission based on the person and work of Jesus Christ, God become flesh. To live at Godspeed is to practice incarnational Christianity.

COCOON, COMBAT, CONFORM

The church has been commissioned in the world to love the very people God loves. We are the apostolic, sent people of God, sent to be on mission and in motion in our immediate contexts for His glory.

Unfortunately, this doesn't usually describe the church. More often than not, our proclivity as Christians is to withdraw from the world, take up arms with the world, or become like the world. In a book called *The Culturally Savvy Christian*, Dick Staub identified these three tendencies as cocooning, combating, and conforming.[1] It's a great alliteration and a great revelation for the church. Let's look at all three.

The first errant tendency Christians have is to cocoon. When we discover how harsh and unfriendly the world can be, our immediate response is to retreat among like-minded company. We set up exclusive Christian clubs and enclaves. Meanwhile, when we see how wonderful Jesus is, we want more than anything to be with Him in heaven. Many Christians talk about this longing all the time, and although the desire is good, Jesus prayed specifically against our feelings of escape. "I do not ask You to take them out of the world,"[2] He said to the Father. God's will until we die is that we would be on mission in the world, among the people of the world for His glory.

We also withdraw and cocoon because the world is tempting. We sense the warfare for our personal holiness and purity, and our reaction is to hunker down. We fail to lay hold of the victory and new nature we've been given through Christ Jesus. For many Christians, personal holiness and purity become the primary goal. But they are not *the* goal—they are *a* goal. Participating in and enjoying the life of Christ is the primary goal of the Christian life.

The second way Christians err is by combating. We are in a battle this side of heaven, there's no doubt about it. But in the midst of that battle the church has to realize that people are not the enemy; people are the prize.

"Our struggle is not against flesh and blood," Paul said, "but against the rulers, against the powers, against the world forces of this darkness, against the spiritual forces of wickedness."[3]

In *UnChristian*, David Kinnaman and Gabe Lyons researched Christianity in America today:

> The primary reason outsiders feel hostile toward Christians, and especially conservative Christians, is not because of any specific theological perspective. What they react negatively to is our "swagger," how

> we go about things and the sense of self-importance we project. Outsiders say that Christians possess bark—and bite. Christians may not normally operate in attack mode, but it happens frequently enough that others have learned to watch their step around us.[4]

That is a tragedy. If people are watching their steps around us, how are we ever going to step into their lives?

Too often the church has set itself up in a purely antagonistic stance. "We are known for having an us-versus-them mentality," wrote Kinnaman and Lyons. "Outsiders believe Christians do not like them because of what they do, how they look, or what they believe. They feel minimized—or worse, demonized—by those who love Jesus."[5]

We've taken the prize, the men and women who need Jesus most, and set them up as our enemies. We've let the fight define us instead of love for people.

The final error Christians make in the world is to conform. We become like the unbelieving world, when Jesus called us to be salt and light.

Salt is only useful when it's salty, and light is only meaningful when it's in contrast to the darkness. Jesus was distinct, and His people should be distinct as well. Romans 12:2 says, "Do not be conformed to this world, but be transformed by the renewing of your mind."

While humanity was hostile to Jesus, He went to them. He then sent you and me *into* the world and asked the Father to protect us from the evil one.[6] When we withdraw from humanity, treat people as the enemy, or conform to the world, we dishonor the teachings of Christ.

DUAL NATURE

Today Christians in America are known as antihomosexual, judgmental, and hypocritical.[7]

That should hit us like a ton of bricks.

Not a single attribute of Christ—loving, compassionate, generous, kind, merciful, humble, caring, or self-sacrificial—makes the list.

The world thinks we're antihomosexual because we're combative. We fought some of the wrong battles on the wrong fronts for the wrong reasons. They think we're judgmental because we cocoon away from them in our little Christian enclaves. They think we're hypocritical because they watch us eventually conform to culture and end up looking like everyone else.

The incarnation of Christ, Jesus in the flesh, must shape the way we live in the world. The reason we're not to cocoon away from people is because Christ came to people. The reason we're not to combat people is because Christ labored to reconcile people, to God and to one another. The reason we're not to conform to this world is because Christ was otherworldly in His character and holiness.

The incarnation of Christ is the model for mission, the example for the Christian living at Godspeed. When Christ took on humanity, He was fully man and yet fully God. "In Him all the fullness of Deity dwells" Colossians 2:9 says, and yet He took on flesh and blood (Heb. 2:14).

Jesus had a dual nature.

Patterned after Jesus, the church also has a dual nature. In John 17, Jesus said we are not of the world because we've been born again as new creations. Then a few verses later, He sent us into the world as members of humanity.[8] *Dual nature.*

Peter called the church a royal priesthood that offers up spiritual sacrifices (worship) and a holy nation that proclaims the excellencies of God (witness).[9] This is what John Stott labeled the double identity of the church,[10] or incarnational Christianity.

Incarnational Christianity means that we're called out of the world in worship to God while being sent into the world as witnesses of God. The church is a worshipping and witnessing community, and Christians are worshipping and witnessing people.

LAME BOAT

Jesus was totally committed to humanity without ever ceasing to be holy, which Stott called "total identification without any loss of identity."[11] This concept is important for those of us who are more committed to humanity than we are to holiness.

Think about boats.

I grew up boating off the coast of Santa Barbara and around the Channel Islands and have spent hundreds of hours fishing and surfing from boats. A boat in the water is so much better than a boat in the front yard, in the driveway, or even on the dock.

Here's when a boat is really lame.

A boat is really lame when water gets inside of it. It's the absolute worst. When the boat fills up with water, it becomes useless to the point that it would have been better to leave the boat in the front yard.

My dad and I used to fish for mako sharks from our boat. Mako sharks are crazy and once on deck they can easily thrash either your body or the boat itself. One time I suggested to my dad that we bring along a shotgun, so we could shoot the shark before we pulled it on board and avoid the thrashing that would result. My dad took one look at me, and I instantly knew what he was thinking … in the heat of the battle with a mako shark there would be as much chance of us blowing a hole in the boat as there would be of blowing a hole in the shark.

Cooler heads prevailed, and we left the gun at home. The thought of the boat filling up with shark-infested water twenty miles out to sea was not a pleasant one.

If you've ever boated, you already know the simple logic of this: you want your boat in the water, but you don't want water in the boat. The same is true for Christians: God wants them in the world, but He doesn't want the world in them.

Maybe this is you right now. Perhaps you're far more committed to humanity than you are to holiness.

Or maybe you err in the opposite way: you're far more committed to holiness than you are to humanity. Perhaps you're a boat that's forgotten why it's a boat.

You're not of the world; *you're out of this world*, so much so that you're not in the world at all anymore. You're too heavenly minded to be of any earthly good for mission, because you've made personal holiness and purity your gods. Some people in the New Testament did this. They were called Pharisees.

Whether we're overly committed to holiness or overly committed to humanity, going too far in either direction is an error because our commitment is to Christ. Jesus, our model, struck the perfect balance. He totally committed His life to humanity without ever ceasing to be holy. He spent time with the broken, the addicted, and the deceitful. He didn't cocoon but stepped into their world, without ever conforming to it.

For those who needed Him most, Jesus was Immanuel, God in their midst. The dual nature of the church is patterned after the dual nature of Christ. He called us to be simultaneously set apart in behavior and sent out in relationship.

NO STRINGS ATTACHED

Because you and I were sent into the world, it follows logic that our most meaningful and fruitful Christian experiences should take place outside the church building.

Many Christians think being on mission in the world is synonymous with inviting people to a church service. It's not the same thing.

Think about this for a minute: we all know people who hate church. Why then is our default strategy to invite them to church?

I don't mean to be overly simplistic, but I think if people liked church, they'd already be at church. We can hope that they'll like it later on, but until then we need a more practical strategy. When people are sick, they don't need an invitation to a church service. They need a Christian who is willing to pray for them, care for them, minister to them, step into their brokenness, and meet their physical needs.

To be on mission is to love people in a way that represents Jesus: God-made-flesh going to humanity.

And we are to do this kind of mission with no strings attached.

Jesus didn't make people go to the synagogue before He fed them, nor after He fed them for that matter. Jesus did mission with no strings attached, but He did it in such a profoundly loving way that His love became inescapable strings to those to whom He ministered.

The prophets Jeremiah and Hosea, along with Paul the apostle, said that God draws us with His love and kindness.[12] These cords that draw humanity to God are the same cords attached to the acts of love we do by His Spirit.

NOT IN CHURCH

As Christians, we invite people to church because we want to introduce them to Jesus. Our underlying assumption here is that Jesus is found at church—that a person will meet Him when they enter the building. We believe Jesus shows up when His body is gathered. This is biblical, but it's not the whole story.

The church hasn't cornered the market on Jesus.

Religion, properly defined, is humanity's efforts to reach and to please God. This is what going to church means for many people.

On the other hand, the incarnation is God's continuing effort to reach and to save humanity. Incarnational Christianity ought to be alive and at work in our world through the people of God, through the church. We ought to be scattered on mission, not gathered all the time.

When we try to get people to Jesus, instead of bringing Jesus to people, we are approaching our faith fundamentally backward.

We're being more religious than Christian.[13] True Christian mission is bringing Jesus to people wherever people are, outside our church buildings.[14]

Also, it doesn't take a math professor to realize all those people "out there" won't fit inside of our church buildings. The Christian concept that we just have to get the world into our buildings is not only incorrect theologically; it doesn't work practically!

We're trying to get the community into church when what we need is to get Jesus into the community. When the church does incarnational Christianity instead of religion, mission becomes more practical.

THE SACRED AND THE SOCCER GAMES

From God's perspective, there's no divide between the sacred and the secular.[15] The incarnation makes this abundantly clear, because when Jesus was born, the sacred invaded the secular—not to destroy it, but to save it, restore it, and renew it.

John Corrie, in the *Dictionary of Mission Theology*, said,

> In the Incarnation of the eternal Word all false dualisms between the material and the spiritual, visible and invisible, human and divine, temporal and eternal, this-worldly and other-worldly, finite and infinite, were dissolved in the totally integrated person of Christ.[16]

Jesus was both fully secular and fully sacred, fully man and fully God. This confronts the unbiblical division we make in our lives when we separate the daily from the divine. We know God cares about the "churchy" stuff, and we think He cares about our problems, but that's where many Christians leave Jesus' involvement.

The truth is, God cares as much about our kids' soccer games as He cares about our churches' Sunday gatherings. Does He not care when the sparrow falls from its nest?[17] And the sparrow never even went to church!

God cares about the details. *Every* detail. And if we truly grasp this fact, it will change the way we live. Life becomes more fun. I've lived both ways to varying degrees: including Jesus in normal life and excluding Him from it as most Americans do. I can hereby testify that life is just more fun with Jesus involved!

I've been trying to lay hold of this concept in my day-to-day life. Recently I went to the park with my dad and two kids, Isaiah and Daisy. We went to the park to fly a little radio-controlled airplane Isaiah got for his birthday. As I sat in the grass watching my family, I let it sink in that God cared as much about that moment as He cares about my moments teaching from the pulpit.

I'll tell you, it made my time in the park that much more amazing. I found myself deeply enjoying the moment, glorifying Jesus, and praying blessings over my family.

As we flew the toy airplane, my dad raced it past a stand of trees, and the thing nearly got stuck in one of them—it's never a good scene when Grandpa loses the birthday present!

Each time the plane launched straight for the treetops, my dad and I called out, "Oh Lord, please no! Jesus, please no!" A little dramatic maybe, but sincere.

And I'm telling you, each time the plane boomeranged around with a *swoosh-plop* moving away from the trees!

Call me crazy, and some surely do, but the Bible shows us that God cares about these little moments. Jesus, *Immanuel*, is with us in each of them.

If we grasp that fact, it will change our lives.

It will change family life, community life, and mission.

NOT EVERY FLIGHT

Now I'm going to take some of the pressure off.

Realizing God cares about all the little moments in life can be overwhelming if we start to manufacture mission. If we think that every time we go to our kid's soccer game we need to feed a hungry person on the sidelines or preach to an unrepentant parent in the stands, the idea of mission will feel overwhelming, even debilitating.

You and I are called to imitate and emulate the life of Christ. Part of this, I believe, includes His capacity to enjoy life.[18] Look at what He talked about in the Gospels: the sparrows, the garden, the marketplace, and His interactions with people. Christ was the creator of all things, which God declared good and created for His pleasure. I can't help but think that Jesus enjoyed incarnational life, and that's part of what it means for us to be God's redeemed people.

In the past I put an awful lot of pressure on myself in this area, thinking that every time I got on an airplane I had to share the gospel with the person sitting next to me—*or I'd be a failure*. There is endless suffering, poverty, and unbelief in the world around us, but every need we see is not an immediate obligation for the Christian. It's the will of Jesus that dictates mission.

One person posted this on our Missio Christi website: "The goal of my daily life is to listen to the Holy Spirit to discover the mission of Christ."

That's right on target.

If Christ says, "Enjoy this time in the park with your kids," then enjoy time in the park with your kids, and may God be glorified in it. If Christ says, "Minister to the needs of this person" or "Proclaim the gospel to that person," then *that* is the thing you should do.

To be sent means to do the will, perform the work, and speak the words of the One who sent us. What we see in the Gospels is that Christ did not heal every leper in Israel. When He ascended, there was still sickness and poverty in the land. Jesus didn't cure every blind man nor heal every lame person.

Ephesians 2:10 reads, "We are His workmanship, created in Christ Jesus for good works, which God prepared beforehand so that we would walk in them." The will of Christ dictates mission because all mission is Christ's mission!

Part of the challenge and the adventure of the Christian life is learning how to listen to the Spirit so we can respond to the needs around us. We have to trust that the Holy Spirit is already working in the lives of people around us, and we need to pay attention to see how and then cooperate with it. If you shift your ministry to be merely need focused, you'll be ruined, discouraged, and utterly overwhelmed.

We're not need driven. We're call driven.

And we're led by the Spirit of God.

UNHOLY PRIVATIZATION

Many of us divide "God stuff" and "my stuff" in our lives. We compartmentalize and privatize faith in our communities, in our homes, and in our hearts.

Jesus never made this separation.

Think of where He spent His time. Do the Gospels typically show Jesus in the temples and the synagogues? In other words, was He most likely to be found at church? Of the fifty-two parables Jesus told, forty-five of them took place in the market context. Of the 132 public appearances Jesus made, 122 of them occurred in the marketplace.

In the mission of Christ, the disciples and the early church followed suit. Of the forty miracles recorded in the book of Acts, thirty-nine of them occurred in the marketplace.[19]

We see in the New Testament that Christ did most of His ministry and mission where people spent most of their time—*at work*. This evidence rings in our ears, because the life of the typical, modern American church is flipped. The place Christ worked most often, in the midst of the culture of the day, is the very place that American Christians have most often evacuated.

Theologian Dallas Willard put it this way:

> There truly is no division between sacred and secular except what we have created. And that is why the division of the legitimate roles and functions of human life into the sacred and secular does incalculable damage to our individual lives and to the cause of Christ. Holy people must stop going into "church work" as their natural course of action

> and take up holy orders in farming, industry, law, education, banking, and journalism with the same zeal previously given to evangelism or to pastoral and missionary work.[20]

Wherever you are now, wherever you spend the majority of your time—that is your mission field. This is what it means to recapture our sense of sent-ness. Wherever you are and whatever you are doing—*you were sent there.*

Sometimes this is hard for American Christians to lay hold of because we've terribly misapplied the concept of separation between church and state. The predominant American mind-set claims little allegiance to religion, and most American Christians see Christianity as an add-on to an already good life. That is a monumental failure, and it messes up mission. It forces us to ask the wrong questions.

We say, "What does God want to do in my life, in my story?"

Incarnational Christianity says, "How can I participate in God's life and greater story?"

The latter question yields a very different result than the former.

Americans claim little allegiance to any religion, and so we easily compartmentalize and privatize our Christian expression. The result is an American church that talks about Jesus only in church.

Many will say that they're unable to talk about Jesus in their workplaces or schools. "I want to be on mission, but it's just not allowed or appropriate."

If this is your reasoning, here's my response: Is that really true? Are you really not allowed to speak about Jesus in your school or at your workplace? Or is this a personal excuse?

If in fact that statement is true—if you are truly not allowed to talk about Jesus at work or school—then my response would be: *awesome*.

What history shows us, and what the world reveals presently, is that the gospel is most fruitful where Jesus is most forbidden. The gospel shines in those places. The less opportunity we have to *talk* about Jesus, the more opportunity we have to *be* like Jesus.

TOUGH IDEAL

The goal is to look like Jesus. And sooner or later, I think every Christian discovers that looking like Jesus is a lot harder to do than it is to say.

Someone posted about this very struggle on our Missio Christi website:

> I understand why it's so much easier for me and for many Christians to just invite people to church rather than to live as a Christian example. I am afraid to try and live as a Christian example. I often fail at it. Non-Christians will put me to shame in how they love and how they treat people in the community. To even match many non-Christians is hard. To surpass them to the point that I'm radiating Christ is an overwhelming prospect. I might be okay twenty-eight days out of the month, but it just takes your non-Christian business associates seeing you those other two days at your worst for them to see a hypocrite and someone who is judgmental rather than loving.[21]

Can anyone relate? I can fully relate. He is absolutely right.

Someone else posted this quote by G. K. Chesterton in response: "The Christian ideal has not been tried and found wanting, it has been found difficult and left untried."[22]

That's where many Christians leave mission. They see it as difficult, and so they leave it untried. When it comes to living out our beliefs, many non-Christians in our communities look a lot more Christian than we do. I know some of them.

But we need to remember two things.

When it comes to God's kingdom and His gospel going forth, we first need to believe that God is bigger than our blunders. Nowhere do we see this more potently than in the history of the church. If you've ever studied church history, you know the church is probably the messiest thing ever to happen to the world. The fact that it still exists and that people are still a part of this worldwide community is concrete proof that God is bigger than our human blunders.

We have to grasp this truth in our daily lives, because the fact is, we are going to blow it. As people, we're deeply flawed; yet throughout history God has chosen to work *through* people rather than *independent of* people.

When we fail, we have an opportunity to model forgiveness and show what the redeeming power of Christ looks like. We can reveal how sweet it is to find our identity in Christ and His work on our behalf because of God's love for us, rather than basing our sense of self-worth on our own performance.

The second thing we have to lay hold of is the power of the gospel. The Christian's good deeds, so to speak, are not merely good deeds. They are purposeful and powerful partnership with God.

That's what it means to be sent: to do the will and the work and to speak the words of the Sender. When we think about speaking and living out the gospel, we're not to see it as a competing ideology or a philosophy in the world. It's the power of God unto salvation,[23] and it works in men and women for transformation.

When we engage in the work of Christ in the world around us—as messy as it is and as bad as we are at it—it yields a different effect in the spiritual realm. If we truly hear what the Spirit is saying and engage in it, there is an impact on the spirits of men and women. The power of God is behind it.

You and I are call driven, not need driven, because Jesus calls us into the work He's already begun—the work that He is faithful to bring to completion. It's Missio Christi.

Whatever Christ does through mission has the power of Christ behind it. The church must rekindle a confidence that the power of the gospel can be communicated through ordinary means: service, sacrifice, kindness, love, and good deeds.[24] Not apart from proclamation but in partnership with it.

The purpose of Ephesians 2:10, the "good works, which God prepared beforehand so that we would walk in them," is to explain our God to the world. And the fact that God already prepared good works for us frees us from having to come up with good ideas and, rather, to seek His ideas.

GOOD POSTMODERN NEWS

The incarnation denotes culture and context. Christ came as a Jew into Jewish culture and participated in Jewish customs with other

Jews. If we're going to do incarnational mission and ministry, we've got to understand some culture and context.

The twenty-first-century American church lives in a postmodern culture.[25] This can be a daunting term, so I want to say a few things about what it means for us.

First, where the modern mind-set was much more concerned with concrete evidence, the postmodern mind-set has shifted. The postmodern mind-set is less concerned with "prove it to me" and much more concerned with "be it to me."

Second, from a postmodern perspective, truth claims are often interpreted as political strategies promoting self-interest.[26] The church must be aware of this distinction, because we make (and need to make) truth claims all the time. Today people have a general suspicion of political maneuvering by those who claim to have the truth, and 75 percent of young, not-yet Christians (ages 16 to 29) see Christians as too political.[27]

Third, postmodernism brings with it a kind of pluralism, the general acknowledgment of diversity. In a rejection of modernism, our pluralistic culture is one where the diversity of racial, religious, ethnic, and cultural groups is not only tolerated but also celebrated. Have you seen the bumper sticker that uses the religious symbols from several different world religions to write the word *coexist*? That's a postmodern, pluralistic perspective. Subsequently four out of five young, not-yet Christians believe Christianity teaches the same basic ideas as the other world religions.[28]

The postmodern mind-set is less concerned with proof and more concerned with fruit; it is suspicious of truth claims as maneuvers for self-interest; it values diversity in all areas of life, including religion.

It rejects exclusiveness and embraces inclusiveness. This mind-set rejects absolute truth, and 76 percent of not-yet Christians in America do not believe absolute truth exists.[29]

This is very bad news for a church that wants to do Christianity as usual. If we're going to be known just for what we are against instead of what we are for, postmodernism is a scary thing.

But I think it's good news.

I think Christ is raising up and calling us to *be* the church, an expression of Christianity that shines His light before people in such a way that they may see our good deeds and glorify our Father who is in heaven.[30] Christ calls us to be a church that speaks the truth in love in order to reach people.[31]

We need to see culture as the opportunity, not the enemy.

We fail if culture is always the enemy.

If you look at the first-century Greco-Roman world, you see it was a pluralistic culture not so different from our own. And what did Christianity do in the first-century world? It spread like wildfire! History tells us that biblical, incarnational mission does very well in a context of pluralism and opposition.

Where modernism was a rejection of God, postmodernism is open to spirituality. And that is a good thing. We live in a culture where more people talk about God and have spiritual conversations. In fact, 82 percent of Americans say they are spiritual seekers, and 52 percent say they've talked about spiritual things in the last twenty-four hours.[32] That's remarkable! Eight out of ten people you'll go to work with tomorrow consider themselves spiritual seekers, and more than half of them are going to have a spiritual conversation during the day.

These conversations are happening all around us.

Are we a part of them?

IMMINENT, EVIDENCED, INTIMATE

Our goal is to get the church into the community in a purposeful, incarnational, meaningful expression, rightly representing Christ through the love that we show people.

We need to go where people need love *and love them*. Our love shouldn't be preconditioned on whether they're ever going to come to church or hear a gospel spiel at that moment. The world has seen enough of this contrived effort and faux befriending. We need to love people authentically, with God's unconditional love. As simple as that sounds, it's really hard to do without being continually tapped into the power of the Holy Spirit.

If Jesus is real in your life and you are real around other people—allowing them to see your failures, successes, struggles, heartaches, heartbreaks, good moments, and worst moments—it won't be long before people see Jesus in you.

We believe in a God who created all things, sustains all things, and participates in all things through personal relationships with those whom He created. We need to gain a greater confidence of Christ's imminence and presence in our lives.

Christ is on mission in the world right now to people all around us. Correct theology liberates us from the old religious thinking that says "I've got to go do things for Jesus" and frees us for incarnational, relational Christianity, which says "I'm going to do things with Jesus."

When we realize that Jesus is doing things in the people all around us, and we get to join with Him in that process, the whole gig changes. "Mission is not first of all an action of ours," Lesslie Newbigin wrote, "it's an action of God, the Triune God, who is unceasingly at work in all creation and in the hearts and minds of all human beings, whether they acknowledge Him or not."[33]

We put flesh on Christ's present mission.

In order to do this mission with Jesus, we first have to be committed to a loving, meaningful, intimate relationship with Him.

Here's why.

If we go to the world before we go to God, we find ourselves going into the world to *get* love instead of to *give* love.

Too many Christians do ministry from a place of their own needs. They do good deeds because it's a part of the identity they want: *I'm that guy who does those things for people. I'm the girl who is always there. I'm the one who saves the day.* Similarly others cultivate relationships because they have love-needs that are yet to be met in their lives—needs designed to be met by Christ alone.

We must become satisfied with and saturated in the love of Jesus. Only then can we go into the world to give love instead of receive love. Only when we do it this way is it the mission of Christ, because the Bible tells us that God is self-sufficient and needs nothing. He did not create us out of need but out of His nature. He did not create us to *get* love from us but to *give* love to us.

Our goal is the same. We must be so satisfied in the love of Christ that we're free to go and give love to others. That doesn't mean that we don't need love. We do. It simply means that we won't be doing mission out of a need to get love from people. Rather, we'll do mission from an overflow of our identity in Christ and the fact that we are the beloved of God. With all of our failures, all of our fissures, all of our brokenness, all of our battles, and all of our drama—we're accepted, adopted, and adored by God.

If we get that identity right in our hearts, then we'll get incarnational Christianity right in the world.

5

SEEK

You Need to Be in Need

Some want to live within the sound of church or chapel bell; I want to run a rescue shop within a yard of hell.

C. T. Studd

A pastor walks into a bar. A gay bar, that is.

Sounds like the beginning of a joke, right?

But a few years ago I was that pastor, and that gay bar was in the heart of downtown Chicago.

High mahogany walls framed a smoke-filled room, and the air was thick with the scent of fresh beer. Everyone in the bar looked comfortable and at ease as they mingled under dim lights. Everyone, that is, except one tan surfer dude from California.

I stuck out like a sore thumb.

I was born and raised in a conservative Christian home in the small town of Carpinteria, California. When I was growing up, I imagine my opinion of homosexuals was similar to that of most small-town, conservative Christians. I viewed the gay community with confusion, fear, a sinful sense of disdain and, at times, even disgust.

I came to Chicago that week with an invitation to study evangelism. One of the very first nights, they sent our study group into the heart of Chicago's gay district to visit bars until dawn to tell people about Jesus. It was way outside the box for a small-town preacher from California.

Awkwardly wandering around the bar, I met a young homosexual woman (who must have taken pity on me), and we struck up a conversation. I don't think I told her too much about Christianity that night—*but I did learn a lot about her.* We sat together into the early-morning hours as she told me her story. She told me about her childhood and her painful past. She told me about her dreams, how she saw herself before God, and what she hoped that her future would hold.

As I listened to her story that night, by the grace of God and for the glory of God, my heart changed. Fear was gone. Disdain and disgust turned to admiration, love, compassion ... and a burden. Hearing that young woman's story forever changed the way I see the world.

Through reading the Gospels, we learn that Jesus truly *knew* people. He knew them supernaturally because He was God—but He also knew them personally, as humanity. Jesus spent time with people, He listened to their stories, and He knew their hearts.

And Jesus certainly didn't wait for people to find Him in the synagogue.

JESUS AND THE WOMAN AT THE WELL

Traveling north from Judea to Galilee, Jesus passed through the land of Samaria. He and the disciples approached a city called Sychar, which sat beside the historical land Jacob gave his son Joseph so many generations before. Sun blazing high overhead, the disciples continued on into the city for food and supplies. Jesus, weary from the journey, sat down by Himself at Jacob's well.

Soon a Samaritan woman walked up to draw water. The culture of the day expected that a man, upon seeing a woman approach, would withdraw by some distance. But Jesus didn't move.

As the Samaritan woman walked up with her bucket, Jesus asked, "Will you give me a drink?"

The woman was stunned.

A Jewish man had spoken to her. More than that, He had asked her for something. "You are a Jew and I am a Samaritan woman," she said, relaying the obvious. "How can You ask me for a drink?"

Jesus looked at her with compassion.

"If you knew the gift of God and who it is that asks you for a drink, you would have asked Him, and He would have given you living water."

The woman was now utterly perplexed.

"Sir, You have nothing to draw with and the well is deep. Where can you get this living water? Are You greater than our father Jacob who gave us the well and drank from it himself, as did also his sons and his livestock?"

But Jesus was no longer speaking of Jacob's well.

He continued. "Everyone who drinks this water will be thirsty again, but whoever drinks the water I give them will never thirst. Indeed, the water I give them will become in them a spring of water welling up to eternal life."

"Sir, give me this water," she responded, "so that I won't get thirsty and have to keep coming here to draw water."

"Go, call your husband and come back."

"I have no husband," she slowly replied.

"You are right when you say you have no husband," Jesus confirmed. "The fact is, you have had five husbands, and the man you now have is not your husband. What you have just said is quite true."

"Sir," she exclaimed, in one of the greatest understatements of the Bible, "I can see that You are a prophet."

The woman then asked Jesus theological questions about worship. With His usual air of mystery, He told her the type of worshippers the Father was seeking.

"I know that the Messiah is coming," she said. "When He comes, He will explain everything to us."

Then Jesus revealed to her the greatest mystery of the world: "I, the one speaking to you, I am He."[1]

MUST NEEDS

This story in John 4 is the first time we see Jesus *pursue* a particular person in the gospel narrative. He demonstrates relational intent toward a Samaritan woman, and His model has immense implications for the modern American church.

The text tells us that Jesus "had to pass through Samaria." The language is strong here, and it's even stronger in the original Greek. What is interesting, however, is that Jesus didn't actually have to go through Samaria. In fact, according to the cultural standards of Judaism, He was expected *not* to go through Samaria.

John 4 says Jesus left Jerusalem and was on His way to Galilee. Geographically Samaria lay smack-dab in the middle of His path. But observant Jews would have crossed over to the eastern side of the Jordan, headed north, and then crossed back over to Galilee once they'd bypassed the region. Jews would go far out of their way to avoid Samaria (and Samaritans) altogether.

When John tells us that Jesus "had to pass through Samaria," something significant is implied. I think the old King James Version makes the interpretation best: Jesus "*must needs* go through Samaria."[2]

I love this language: *must needs*. I use it all the time when I want something: "Must needs food. I must needs to go surfing." What a great biblical phrase! I'm sure my wife loves it too.

John says that Jesus must needs pass through Samaria, even though it's counter to His culture and flies in the face of His religious peers. In the Greek, *must needs*, also translated "it was necessary for Him to" or "He had to," implies that because of the nature of the situation, the act is absolutely necessary.

What was the nature of Jesus' situation? Was His decision geographic or theocentric? Did He travel through Samaria for convenience's sake or for mission's sake?

Later on in Luke 19:10, Jesus explained, "The Son of Man has come to seek and to save that which was lost." The word *seek* implies something that is not readily accessible or attainable. Throughout the Gospels, we see Jesus constantly and consistently *seeking* lost people.

But were the lost hard to find?

WE DON'T SHARE CUPS

In every country across the globe, missionaries work exhaustively to understand the cultural barriers that prevent the progress of the gospel. They seek to know the barriers of language, tradition, and worldview. Every missionary must develop an acute understanding of these factors in their mission field and strategically work to reach the people in their midst.

You or I may never set foot outside this country as a missionary, but each of us is just as much a missionary wherever we live. Like missionaries in other cultures and countries, we must recognize and seek to understand the barriers to the gospel around us. These barriers prevent the people we love, and the people we meet, from hearing the message of the gospel.

For Jesus, the lost were never hard to find. But barriers prevented them from coming to Him, so He had to *seek* people in order to reach them. Sin, of course, is the greatest barrier between God and humanity. But issues of culture, identity, race, sexuality, and social taboos kept people in Jesus' day from hearing His message of eternal life. These barriers are on overt display in the story of Jesus and the woman at the well.

Jesus, we know, was a Jew. The woman was a Samaritan.

Before a word was said, there was cause for tension.

Samaria was the region that ran between Jerusalem and Galilee on the west side of the Jordan River—what we now know as the West Bank. Samaritans live there to this day, and you can still visit Jacob's well. The word *tension* is far too weak a word to describe the volatile racial and religious issues that existed between the Jews and the Samaritans of Jesus' time. This seemingly irreconcilable hatred had existed between these neighboring people groups for over five hundred years when Jesus met the woman at the well. As Americans, we can hardly fathom the depth and history of this conflict.

This situation makes a lot more sense when we understand the history of Samaria, so here's the *Reader's Digest* version.

Over seven hundred years before Jesus was born, the Assyrians invaded both the northern part of Israel and the region of Samaria. They conquered the world, you could say. The Assyrians captured and relocated some Jews from the Samarian region, and they also planted a population of their own people among the Jews in Samaria. Once a new social order settled in, the Jews of Samaria did something prohibited by Jewish law: *they began to intermarry with the Assyrians.*

A couple hundred years later, in 586 BC, a similar situation occurred during the conquest of the Babylonians. Babylonian armies invaded the southern kingdom of Jerusalem, exiling Jews and planting their own people as the Assyrians had done. But unlike the Jews of Samaria in the north, the Jews of the south held firmly to the law. They refused to intermarry.

Years later, after everyone had returned to the land, the Jews in the southern kingdom determined that the Jews in the northern kingdom had compromised. Beyond intermarriage, the Jewish Samaritans had taken on elements of the pagan Assyrian religion and began practicing syncretism. The Samaritans had compromised racially and religiously, and the defection was so extreme that the rabbis of Jerusalem declared all Samaritans unclean—*all the time.*

This is why pious Jews did not pass through Samaria. If they did so, they would be considered religiously impure and prohibited from participating in the religious life of Israel. A popular Jewish prayer of the day went, "And Lord, do not remember the Samaritans in the resurrection." Or in less euphemistic terms, "Lord, let them be damned forever."

Across history the two groups warred against each other. In Luke 9, the Samaritans commanded the disciples to leave town when they tried to travel through Samaria. How did the disciples respond? They turned to Jesus and asked, "Do You want us to command fire to come down from heaven and consume them?"[3] In other words, "Jesus, can we kill them?"

The racial, geographic, and religious hatred between Jews and Samaritans was palpable. In John 4:9, a parenthetical statement adds, "For Jews have no dealings with Samaritans." In the Greek, this text literally means "we don't share cups."

No wonder the Samaritan woman was shocked when a Jewish rabbi asked her for a drink.

WE'VE GOT ISSUES

The night before I shared this message with our church, I clicked on the headline news for a moment. That day violence had erupted on the Temple Mount in Israel: Arabs and Palestinians had thrown rocks at Jews and tourists, and the Jewish police had responded with force and waves of tear gas.

The hatred and division of cultures from Jesus' day is still an unceasing reality of life in the Middle East. This type of tension shows up in our own backyards in America as well. The effects are often less overt, but the issues are just as real.

In my hometown on the California coast, 50 percent of our community is Hispanic. Yet when I look closely, I notice that we don't live in the same neighborhoods. We don't eat at the same restaurants, and we don't shop at the same stores. We don't wave when we're driving past each other, and we don't look one another in the eye when we're walking down the street. More accurately, I realized we actually walk down different streets. Within my own community, true racial tensions exist, and these are barriers to the gospel.

Racial and religious barriers are some of the most difficult to cross because they are held most sacred.

Here's another major boundary that Jesus obliterated: have I emphasized yet that the Samaritan at the well was a *woman*? Jesus was alone at the well in the middle of the day when the woman approached the well by herself. According to the culture of the day, it was absolutely inappropriate for them to talk. But here was Jesus, not only a man but also a Jewish rabbi, discussing theological issues with a woman. When the disciples returned to the scene later in the chapter, they were more than surprised—they were downright upset.[4]

Gender issues in our culture today are radically different, but they are equally significant. Sex changes, for example, have become a normalized, and at times celebrated, part of our society—yet women statistically get paid less than men for the same professional positions. Society insists on paying the sexes different wages for the same work, but you can change your sex at any time if you so choose. In some ways I think we are more confused about sexual identity than the culture of Jesus' day.

The majority of all barriers ultimately boils down to issues of identity: the ways in which others perceive us and the ways in which we see ourselves.

The Samaritan woman was alone at the local well at noon. Normally women went to the well only in the mornings and the evenings, both to avoid the blistering heat of the day and to replenish water during the times when they would need it most.[5] The women always went to the well in groups, never by themselves.[6] So why was the Samaritan woman violating so many social norms?

Water was a commodity everyone needed in that day; comparative to the way our culture relies on coffee. The well was like your local Starbucks, and you could count on the regulars you would run into there. The Samaritan woman was alone at the well in the middle of the day because she had intentionally removed herself from community. She was ashamed of her lifestyle, had been ostracized by the other women, and didn't want to see anybody she knew.

Jesus directly addressed the woman's five marriages. Surely her divorces had caused immense relational brokenness, and she currently lived with another man in an immoral relationship. This lifestyle wasn't normal in Jesus' culture the way it is today, and her community rejected her as a result. This woman approached the well at noon, when the peak watering times were morning and evening, and she came alone, when most women would come in groups. She was an outcast in the community. In this moment she must have felt ashamed, second-best, less-than, and unworthy.

Each of us can understand, to some degree, such feelings of brokenness—from divorces to broken families, sexual issues to full-fledged abuse. These are the kinds of wounds that Jesus came to heal.

Had Jesus not been intentional in a few very significant ways, these racial, religious, relational, sexual, and identity barriers would have kept a Samaritan woman from meeting her Savior.

NO BUCKET, NO BOAT—NO PROBLEM

Every time I read the story of Jesus and the woman at the well, I am amazed at Jesus' obvious oversight. He sat by the well in the middle of the day *with no bucket*.

Now I'm confident that Jesus and the disciples would have owned a bucket. Every traveling group in the day had a leather bucket they carried with them at all times.[7] But when the disciples went into town to buy food, apparently Jesus intentionally let them take the bucket with them.

The text tells us that Jesus was tired and thirsty. He had put Himself in a position—part circumstantial, part intentional, but all providential—where He needed the woman who would come His way.

By positioning Himself in a place of need, Jesus was able to break every radical, deep-seated, and centuries-old barrier with four simple words: "Give me a drink."

Suddenly the woman was needed; the woman was valuable. Jesus humbled Himself to the point of actually needing the very person He came to reach.

You'll remember that one of Jesus' early interactions with Peter was similar. Jesus stood on the shore of the Sea of Galilee preparing to preach, but the horde of waiting people pushed Him up against the water's edge.

He called out, "Peter, I need your boat!" Then He instructed the fisherman to row out from the shore and hold steady.[8] In order to accomplish His mission in that moment, Jesus legitimately needed Peter—a man who would become one of the greatest apostles in history. Peter's mission began with Jesus asking for help with a practical need. Christ embodies such radical humility that He put Himself in a position to need the people He came to save.

Christians are known for perpetuating the myth that they have to have it all together all the time. But God purposefully entrusted the treasure of His gospel—*the living water*—to jars of clay.

You and I are broken, earthen vessels, and He chose us to show that power comes from Him alone.[9] Our calling then is to share this gospel, not to achieve some level of societal perfection. In order to live our lives at Godspeed and with gospel intentionality, we will have to learn to give *and* receive. Most of us are aware that we have something to give. Now we must learn that we have something to receive while living on mission with Christ.

When Jesus brought His simple need to this woman, it instantly elevated her sense of self-worth. She had been ashamed and ostracized, relationally and sexually broken, but suddenly she was genuinely needed. Jesus could have turned the desert sand into a stream of water, but He chose instead to lift her up.

Genuine relationships form when there is mutual need between two people. I love the way one longtime missionary put it: "The only way to build love between two people, or two groups of people is to be so related to each other as to stand in need of each other."[10]

Marriage, by design, is the perfect illustration of this relationship by mutual need. As long as both partners have legitimate, God-given need for each other—and seek to meet each other's needs—the marriage will flourish. Conversely, divorce occurs when one or both spouses say, "I don't need you anymore." This principle is equally applicable between races, genders, and people groups. When one party says, "We don't need you," radical divisions open up.

God designed relationships to thrive on mutual need. When we place ourselves in settings of mutual need, we discover that barriers are brought down, relationships develop, and opportunities to communicate the gospel naturally appear.

Last year someone stole my friend Bob's car. Actually this had happened to him twice in quick succession. But this time, instead of cashing in the insurance money, he decided to go without a car for a while.

Bob is one of the most successful lawyers I know, and he realized there wasn't much he needed from his friends and family anymore. By not having a car, Bob needed people again. He needed his employees to pick him up, his friends to lend him their cars, and his kids to give him rides home. In needing people, Bob was able to love on his community, and he looked a lot like Jesus in the process.

And for the days when a car wasn't available?

Bob taught himself to ride a skateboard. And he's not particularly young!

A NEW HUMILITY

When Jesus met the woman at the well, He was on His way out of Jerusalem to avoid conflict with the Pharisees, who were condemning and denouncing His ministry. Jesus entered the situation as a person who had just been rejected.

Jesus didn't wait for the Samaritan woman to find Him in Jerusalem, where she would have been further ostracized and discriminated against. Rather, on the heels of being cast out Himself, He went to the place where He was the social minority and put Himself in legitimate need before her.

Too often as Christians we wait for evangelism to happen at church. We expect the not-yet Christians to come to us. Is this really biblical or even prudent? Jesus met the Samaritan woman in her own context. For many people, church represents a place where they feel out of place, discriminated against, and misunderstood.

So how do we begin to take the gospel *to* them?

In Mark 10:45, Jesus characterized Himself when He said, "The Son of Man did not come to be served, but to serve, and to give His life as a ransom for many." If we care for people from a place of power, we aren't servants—*we're benefactors.*[11] Jesus modeled servitude, and a servant, to some degree, must be in need, must depend upon other people. This is why Jesus came as a babe and not as a king.

When we look at the life of Jesus, our model, we see that while the foundation of mission is the glory of God, the basis for all mission is *humility*.

The book of Philippians says Jesus surrendered His divine privileges, was born a babe, took on the position of a slave, and humbled Himself to the point of death on a cross.[12] The humility of Jesus is so essential to the life of faith that we cannot join His mission without this same humility. You and I will never effectively participate in the mission of Christ unless, by the grace of God and by the work of the Holy Spirit, we develop a deep and authentic humility.

We are called to be servants like Jesus. He attempted to build this humble character into the lives of His disciples, and He's also trying to build it into your life and my life. Sending the disciples on their first mission trip in Mark 6, Jesus instructed them, "Take nothing for the journey except a staff—no bread, no bag, no money in your belts."[13]

From the outset, Jesus put His disciples in need of the people to whom He sent them.

This concept is hard for us—*very hard*. As Americans, we never want to need others; it's seen as weakness. Perhaps this is why ministry and mission happen so much more easily when we go overseas. Foreign places make us the lost and confused minority, and we're instantly in need of the people to whom we've come to minister. Our dependency on the locals immediately breaks down barriers for the gospel.

Can we begin to live this way in our own backyards?

For most of us, Christlike humility doesn't come naturally. This humility in us must be molded through the teachings of Scripture and then refined by the circumstances God allows into our lives.

My daughter's battle with cancer the past couple of years has caused me to need people in ways I've never experienced before. During the battle, I wasn't always able to minister to others. In fact, I needed someone to minister to me. Our family was no longer in a position to give to others—we needed someone to give to us.

This year my family needed the body of Christ, and we needed not-yet Christians. Having no control of our circumstances, each week we sat before doctors and nurses on whom we desperately depended to guide us through this journey. In the midst of the darkest and most tumultuous season of our lives, God gave us the opportunity to demonstrate His love to the people we needed. I learned firsthand the kind of humility that works in our lives when we allow ourselves to need other people.

STORY-HEARING

To the not-yet Christian world, Christians today look a lot like a Jewish rabbi must have looked to a Samaritan woman. When Jesus approached, surely the woman's mind flooded with preconceptions about why He didn't like her, why she didn't like Him, and why they should both keep their distance.

Modern Christians are seen as antihomosexual, judgmental, and hypocritical. As the woman at the well saw a Jew and thought about racial issues, religious issues, and gender issues, many people today see Christians and think about sexual issues, lifestyle issues, and consistency issues.

All of these are barriers to the gospel.

The church has a tendency to blame the media for negative stereotypes of Christianity. We assume that the news agencies cast us in a bad light and that the follies of Christian leadership frame public misconceptions. Yet studies show that most young, not-yet Christians actually form their perceptions of Christianity through conversations with people and not the media.[14] And usually those conversations are with Christians.

What's at stake here is not the public's opinion of you or me personally. The thing that matters is what people think about Jesus.

The bad news is that their conversations with us have led people to think we're antihomosexual, judgmental, and hypocritical—all of which are a misrepresentation of Jesus. But the *good news* is that people are, in fact, affected by our conversations with them. This means we have a unique opportunity and a great responsibility to enter into dialogue with people. Jesus had conversations with people—even deep theological dialogues, like His discussion with the woman at the well. In humility, Jesus positioned Himself in ways that were conducive to conversation.

I never would have walked into a Chicago gay bar that night on my own, but the training program sent me there to seek people. As a Christian surfer from a small town in California, I was absolutely the minority, and I definitely felt out of place. Looking back, I realize I needed someone to befriend *me*. I will never forget the friendship of the young woman I spoke to that night or the way that conversation shaped my heart.

When we take the time to hear one another's stories, those experiences change the way we feel about each other and the way we do mission. It didn't change my theology. I believed then and I believe now that homosexuality is a sin. I think Jesus did too. It did however change my heart toward people. I'm not afraid of, nor do I disdain, people who are homosexual. I love them. I know Jesus does too.

We live in a world where cultural values collide with biblical morals on a colossal scale each day. As the church, we are called to address this collision with the gospel and to love the people in our midst.

How much better could we live out this calling if we took the time to really know people? If we learned the backgrounds of those struggling with big moral problems and heard the stories of those most affected by the social issues of our day? I don't know if it would make the answers to these issues any clearer, but it would make loving each other easier. And maybe that is the answer.

Throughout the Gospels, we see Jesus keeping the company of the people considered "the worst" by society's standards. This was one of the favorite accusations of the religious leaders against Him.

Jesus went into people's homes, He ate meals with them, and He lingered long with them around the table. I imagine everyone He met, from the poorest prostitutes to the wealthiest tax collectors, had the chance to tell Jesus their stories.

Did you know that most non-Christians today think you and I view them as projects? Only one out of every three people believe that Christians genuinely care about them.[15] No matter how hard we try to share the gospel, it will always be true humility and mutual need that move us from being project oriented to relationship oriented with the people we're called to reach. Humility and need enable us to demonstrate authentic love like Jesus did.

THE NEW EVANGELIST

Jesus *knew* the Samaritan woman. He knew her past and current sin, yet He broke down barriers to seek her out. The disciples wouldn't have been caught dead with her (they probably would have tried to call down fire again), but Jesus knew something you and I also often forget:

Those who are forgiven much, love much.

At the end of the day, most people don't need us to tell them we disapprove of their lifestyles. They usually understand this already. Jesus did not condone the lifestyle choices of the woman at the well, and He clearly addressed her sin—as He always did. But Jesus demonstrated that we don't need to condone people's behavior in order to love them. Romans 5:8 explains, "God demonstrates His own love toward us, in that while we were yet sinners, Christ died for us." When we were at our worst, God demonstrated the greatest act of love.

Humanity would have never understood or experienced the love of God had Jesus not given up certain divine rights, made Himself a servant, and suffered on a cross. No one has ever seen God in all His glory, but Jesus embodies His nature.[16] God is love, and He breaks down barriers to seek the lost.

This is why Jesus *must needs* pass through Samaria. You and I, as redeemed image bearers of God living after the model of Jesus, must always seek to identify and break down barriers in a similar way. The love of God compels us.[17]

Do you know what the Samaritan woman did immediately after her encounter with Jesus?

If you read the end of the chapter, John says she went into the city and told the local men about Jesus. Instantly she confronted the gender barrier, and the Bible says that the men listened and *believed her*.[18] This was a time when a woman's testimony wasn't even allowed in a court of law, and yet there she was, the first female evangelist.

The text says that because of this woman's testimony, many Samaritans came to listen to and believe in Jesus. Once an outcast woman, she confronted gender barriers, cultural barriers, religious barriers—and many in her community were saved as a result.

Like the woman at the well, you and I have encountered and been changed by the love of God through Jesus Christ. Now we must follow Jesus and break down every barrier to share this good news with the world.

6

TOUCH

It's Gonna Get Messy

Preach the gospel at all times.
When necessary, use words.
Saint Francis of Assisi

Do you remember the swine flu epidemic?

I remember it vividly because I came down with it. I caught the virus right in the middle of Daisy's chemotherapy treatments, and there couldn't have been a worse time for me to get sick.

When someone goes through chemotherapy, his or her immune system is extremely compromised. As chemo kills the rapidly producing cancer cells, it also knocks out every other rapidly producing cell in the body (hair cells, for example). Most dangerous of all, chemo kills off the white blood cells that create and sustain the body's immune system, leaving a chemo patient incredibly susceptible to viruses.

As you can imagine, my illness created a pretty serious situation in our home. At the command of the head physician (my wife), I was immediately quarantined to the back of our house until I got well. And I mean *quarantined.* I was put in the very last room at the end of the hall, and the door was shut—*and that was that.*

Quarantine was bearable at first, until the days started crawling by. I found myself literally aching to hold my wife and kids. As a very touchy-feely family, we're always hugging each other, kissing each other, sitting on each other, and holding each other. By the fifth day in, I was going absolutely mad without Isaiah, Daisy, and Kate.

I longed for their touch.

After a couple of weeks in total isolation without significant contact with my wife and kids, I couldn't stand it any longer. My bout with swine flu had taught me how important it is to be touched.

Jesus, knowing the deepest needs of humanity, intentionally incorporated touch into mission.

JESUS AND THE LEPER

After traveling throughout the region of Galilee, preaching in the synagogues and driving out demons, Jesus stopped in the middle of a town and began to teach. Having heard rumors of this Jewish rabbi, a large crowd gathered around to hear Him speak.

Jesus was in the middle of sharing a parable when suddenly the crowd stirred. People gasped and staggered back, horrified, as a leper pushed his way to the front. Falling to his knees before Jesus, the man begged Him, "If You are willing, You can make me clean."

Rocked with compassion, Jesus stretched out His hand, touched the man, then said, "I am willing; be cleansed."

Immediately every sign of the man's disease disappeared. The crowd gazed in awe upon a man, once full of leprosy, now fully healed.[1]

Leprosy is one of the most painful diseases known to man, though ironically it numbs the body from actually feeling physical pain. A "painless hell" one doctor called it.[2] Leprosy is painful because it is a disease of sensory deprivation. Lepers might wash their faces with scalding water because they cannot sense the temperature or grip a tool so tightly that the blade cuts to the bone. The inability to feel pain literally destroys the body of the diseased individual.

Can you imagine being physically unable to experience touch? What it would be like to reach out to someone and feel no sensation in the contact?

A pastor I admire once wrote about a man he counseled. The man was not a Christian, and he felt incredibly broken and lonely. He had no family that cared about him, no church body to call his own, and no real friends to speak of. In describing his loneliness to the pastor, the man revealed that every week he would pay for a haircut—just so somebody would *touch* him.[3] He was desperate for a thing God created us to need and desire.

Touch is a legitimate need, designed by God. When rightly expressed, it is a powerful conduit for good in humanity. Conversely the power of touch is evidenced in its ability to be applied in evil ways, such as violence, physical abuse, and sexual abuse. Each of those evil acts is a wicked perversion of our God-ordained need.

Touch is powerful.

The leper who met Jesus went without one of the most basic human needs due to the alienation caused by his disease. The account in Luke says that the man was full of leprosy—meaning that his disease was far advanced.[4] This man had not been touched in a very, very long time.

As horrific as leprosy is physically, its social implications in first-century Judaism were infinitely worse. Leviticus 13 describes the difficult laws that God gave Israel to protect the general health of the community:

> As for the leper who has the infection, his clothes shall be torn, and the hair of his head shall be uncovered, and he shall cover his mustache [his mouth] and cry, "Unclean! Unclean!" He shall remain unclean all the days during which he has the infection; he is unclean. He shall live alone; his dwelling shall be outside the camp.[5]

The implications of these words are heartbreaking. The leper was unclean, he lived alone, and he stayed outside the camp. By law, the leper ruined his clothes in order to identify his ailment, and anytime he was around people, he had to yell out his infirmity for all to hear. I don't think we can fathom the humiliation experienced by the leper in this context.

Leviticus 13 also says that if someone's skin showed the beginnings of leprosy, the law required the person to consult a priest immediately. The priest would make the determination, and if it was in fact leprosy, he would directly quarantine the individual. The new leper would be removed quickly from his or her community, friends, and family, exiled completely, and forced to live alone.

Imagine the experience of a father suddenly diagnosed with leprosy. This man, with a wife and children whom he loved, would be cast out at a moment's notice with the knowledge that he would never touch his sweet family again. I imagine this man standing on the hill overlooking his home, watching his children play in the streets, seeing his wife return home alone from the well every evening.

It sounds like a nightmare.

If this man ever came near people, he'd have to cover his mouth and yell out, "Unclean! Unclean!" His leprous voice would be disfigured like his body, as the disease even affects the vocal cords. What was once the loving voice of a father would now scrape and rumble, like some sort of monster, as he called out his horrific affliction: "Unclean! Unclean!"

In panic, men, women, and children would run from the sound.

STIGMATIZED

Believe it or not, pop star Katy Perry attended our youth group in Santa Barbara many years ago. Recently I saw the music video for her hit single "Firework." The video interweaves snapshots of young people who have been stigmatized by their community: a boy who is gay, a teen girl who is uncomfortable with her weight, siblings living with abusive parents. I was struck when one of the featured characters was, like my daughter, a cancer patient.

A stigma is a mark of disgrace somehow associated with a person or his or her circumstance.[6] We may not require people with ailments to call out "Unclean!" as they walk down our streets today, but as Perry's video illustrates, stigmas remain a very real influence in our society.

As students of the Word of God and people in God's world, it is our challenge to read the Gospels in historical context and apply them to present-day circumstances. Who then, we must ask, bears a stigma in our society? Who has been declared socially unclean or carries a mark of disgrace?

The answer to this question may be different for the Christian than it is for the rest of society. Some people have been stigmatized by broader American culture: Muslims, for example, after the terrorist attacks on September 11. Meanwhile, there are many people whom Christians have stigmatized in some way, and they're not interested in Christianity as a result. In casting sinners out with their sins, the church has left a lot of broken people in its wake.

On the other hand, the church is often stigmatized by the world. I am saddened to meet so many believers today who are embarrassed to call themselves "Christian" for this reason. A web of connectivity exists between stigmas that reflect and refract human brokenness. The church stigmatizes the world, and the world stigmatizes the church. The result is a separated and segregated society.

The leper was forced to broadcast the stigma that society had placed upon him. When we carry these stigmatized labels long enough, they change our identities.

When I was a child, my mom frequently said that if you tell people they are something for long enough, they will eventually begin to believe you. At the time, I had a long list of horrible names I called my little sister—"Ugly … Stupid … Troll"—and I used every other terrible, hurtful name a big brother could know.

"If you tell her that long enough, she will eventually think it's true," my mother warned me. Being stubborn and rebellious, I didn't believe her then.

I see how very right she was today.

As a pastor, I've met too many girls who have developed eating disorders because at some point they were scrutinized for their looks. And I've known too many men who have spent their adulthoods believing they will never measure up because an authority figure, years ago, told them they weren't good enough.

I still remember the first time I ever played a song on the guitar for someone, having just learned. Immediately he said, "That doesn't sound like 'Hotel California'!" To this day, decades later, no matter what I play on the guitar, it never sounds like I think it's supposed to sound. I still believe that I cannot play the guitar well.

If we label people according to stigmas, eventually we will believe that the negative connotations of those stigmas are true. Worse yet, if we verbalize and socialize those stigmas, the people we stigmatize will begin to believe those labels about themselves.

AS GOOD AS DEAD

When the leper met Jesus, he felt wholly unworthy, entirely unwanted, and incapable of feeling or receiving touch. The law required his removal from society, and Jewish rabbis of the day only exacerbated his misery.

Jewish religious leaders taught that if a leper so much as stuck his head inside a house, the entire home would be unclean. These leaders made it illegal to greet a leper, so an observant Jew couldn't even say hello. If a leper was upwind from another person, rabbinical law said that he or she must remain at least 150 feet away.[7]

"When I see lepers," wrote one Jewish rabbi, "I throw stones at them, lest they come near me." In Luke 17, a group of ten lepers stood a distance away from Jesus, because they didn't know if He, as a Jewish rabbi, would throw stones at them.[8]

The woman at the well had culpability for her five divorces and her sexual immorality. She had made decisions that contributed to her marginalization from community. But the tragedy of the leper was that his marginalization and rejection came for reasons entirely beyond his control. The leper was a victim, in the truest sense of the word, and yet his culture didn't view him as such. Ignorantly, some Jewish people believed that lepers had been cursed by God and were therefore deserving of their fate. More than any other individual, the leper of the day was a casualty of the sin of humanity.

The Old Testament laws given to protect Israel from infectious diseases were good, but the implications—and the way people applied them—were horrible. The leper was ruined socially, economically, physically, emotionally, and religiously. He was totally isolated, totally humiliated.

According to the Jewish historian Josephus, lepers were treated as though they were already dead.[9]

Judaism taught that God alone could heal leprosy, a miracle second only to someone being raised from the dead.[10] Even the New Testament authors viewed the healing of lepers differently because of the social stigma involved. In Matthew 10, the disciples were told to "heal the sick, raise the dead, cleanse the lepers, cast out demons."[11] Lepers had their own category of redemption. Beyond a healing, the leper's miracle was total cleansing of the social stigma: the idea that they were dirty, outcast, and unwelcome.

The Bible speaks of us this way in 1 Corinthians 6, when it talks about the gravity of our identity as sinners. "But you were cleansed," it continues. "You were sanctified."[12] Once, we were as unclean as the leper, but by Jesus' blood we are made clean.

When a leper was cleansed and restored to community by Jesus, it was evidence of the coming of the kingdom of God.[13]

GUT-WRENCHING

I've not described the physical horrors of leprosy because that, I believe, is best left to Google's image search. Spend just a moment on Google's search page, and you will see that the leper was a desperate man. In pushing through the crowd to meet Jesus, he broke every social, cultural, religious, and medical barrier that existed. His desperation was most acutely displayed in his bold approach to Jesus.

The account in Matthew explains that a multitude of people followed Jesus at the time.[14] We see the leper didn't call out the mandatory "Unclean! Unclean!" nor maintain the required upwind distance of 150 feet. In true desperation, he pushed through the crowd and fell at Christ's feet and began to plead. The passage even implies that the leper grabbed hold of Jesus.[15]

Everything the leper did was unacceptable, but he was driven by a belief that somehow Jesus could cleanse him.

"If You are willing," he said to Jesus, "You can make me clean."

The leper was absolutely sure that Jesus had the power to heal him … but he wasn't sure if Jesus was *willing*. Because of the stigma, because of the rejection, because religious culture said that leprosy was a curse from God, the leper did not know if Jesus would cleanse him. He knew Jesus represented the power of God, but he was unsure what the heart of God toward him would be.

Do you know how many people there are, both inside the church and outside church walls, who feel the same way? They are convinced that Jesus cleanses, and they are certain that Jesus forgives, but they are unsure as to whether or not Jesus will cleanse and forgive *them*. They see themselves as untouchable or as beyond the redemption of God.

Mark 1:41 says that Jesus was "moved with compassion" by the leper's plea. We see this over and over again in the Gospels. Jesus is moved with compassion for leaderless crowds, those like sheep without a shepherd. He also feels compassion for the hungry, the bereaved, the blind, the marginalized, and especially the sick.[16]

The phrase "moved with compassion" goes beyond simple pity. Jesus did not pity the leper. His reaction went beyond any level of sympathy or empathy.

The phrase used in the original Greek means that Jesus was literally moved in His inner being when He saw the leper.

Jesus felt gut-wrenching compassion for this man.

SUFFERING WITH

We all know the saying "misery loves company." Humanity deals best with suffering when in community, and the Bible makes this intrinsic to the calling of the church.

"Weep with those who weep," says Romans 12:15. Yet the leper's condition radically limited his ability to build relationships. The leper didn't just suffer—he suffered alone.

After the operation to remove Daisy's first cancerous tumor, her pain was so unbearable that the doctors decided to give her an epidural. They also gave her morphine and another heavy painkiller, but even after all that medication, her pain was still excruciating.

There was nothing we could do to lessen my five-year-old daughter's suffering, and to add to it, she developed bedsores. Daisy couldn't bear the thought of us moving her body and would whimper for us not to touch her. When we lifted her up to reposition her on the bed, she would scream in pain.

This does something in the guts of a dad. In the most real and perceptible way, you suffer with your child.

Hebrews 4:15 states that Jesus is touched with the feeling of our infirmities. Psalm 34:18 says, "The LORD is near to the brokenhearted and saves those who are crushed in spirit."

In ways we cannot fathom, our heavenly Father suffers with us in our pain. This knowledge alone helps us to cope with the suffering we see around us in the world.

Our God suffers with us. But more than that, our God suffered *for* us. On the cross, Jesus died a substitutionary death during which He literally felt the depths of our pain. Jesus took upon Himself the weight of our sin and all its implications. He bore our grief and carried our sorrows, and in suffering on our behalf, He realized the truest realities of our hurts.[17]

The pain of the leper was real to Christ. Surely Jesus could have healed the man with a word, for He had healed others who were sick from great distances. But Jesus felt the magnitude of this man's pain, so He stretched out His hand to touch him. How long had it been since someone had touched this man?

Jesus, as God and as a man, touched the untouchable.

In ancient Jewish culture, this act was unthinkable. The experience with the woman at the well paled when compared to a Jewish rabbi touching a person with leprosy. By touching this man, Jesus had made Himself unclean and susceptible to the disease.

The crowd and the disciples were horrified.

Jesus disregarded the Old Testament rules, but it's not to say He had a low view of the law. Jesus elevated the law in the Sermon on the

Mount, and He held a higher view of the law than any other human ever had (or ever will) in history.

But Jesus had His priorities straight.

He knew the law wasn't given to perpetuate suffering, so He chose to touch the leper and heal him. In Mark 1:44, Jesus told the man to show himself to the priest and offer a sacrifice, thereby obeying the law's command.

Jesus had no vendetta against religious rules.

But people were His priority.

THE SWEETNESS OF SOUL

During the Middle Ages, Saint Francis of Assisi made a confession in his last testament, revealing the point of life at which he finally felt "that sweetness of soul."

It happened as he rode his horse one day and encountered a leprous beggar on the road. It was a horrific sight for the saint, and immediately he turned his horse and spurred it hard in the other direction.

As he rode away from the leper, Saint Francis suddenly felt an overwhelming sense of remorse. Having turned away from his brother's need, he realized he galloped away from God, who suffers in every man's suffering. Whipping his horse around, Saint Francis charged back toward the leper. When he came upon the man, he dismounted, fell on his knees before the beggar, and began kissing the man's leprous hand. After that day, the saint's life was never the same.[18]

The question for us is this: *Are we willing to suffer with those who are suffering?*

To do mission like Christ is to put our hands on the rotting flesh of humanity, wherever we find it. Both Matthew 11 and Luke 7 make it evident that when lepers are cleansed, the kingdom has come.[19] By touching and cleansing the leper, Jesus demonstrated what He taught throughout all of Galilee.[20]

So often today we see conservative Christians proclaiming the gospel but failing to demonstrate it. We see liberal Christians demonstrating the gospel but failing to proclaim it.

Jesus always did both.

He proclaimed that the kingdom was coming, and then He demonstrated the coming of that kingdom. In being sent in the way Jesus was sent, the church must balance *both* radical proclamation *and* radical demonstration of the gospel. Jesus was always both/and in His approach.

In areas of social justice and ministries of mercy, the church should lead the way. We must work on the cutting edge of caring for the poor, the orphans, and the widows. The world should know us for our outreach to the destitute and our provision for the needy.

But the church should never do these ministries instead of proclaiming the gospel. As John Piper has often said, "Jesus is concerned about eliminating all suffering, *especially* eternal suffering."

WHO TOUCHED WHO?

By touching the leper, Jesus demonstrated what He had proclaimed—namely that He is the One who makes all things new.

Throughout the Old Testament, we see that if a person came in contact with something or someone who was unclean, they too were made unclean. If they touched something that was unholy, they too were made unholy.

The opposite was never true—*until Jesus*.

In Christ, the unclean become clean by touching the clean. By the power of Jesus, the kingdom of God is one of reversal.

UNFASHIONABLE

I want to challenge you to read a disturbing passage in Matthew 25, beginning with verse 31. Jesus spoke of a day of judgment and warned the crowd of the two groups that every person will fall in to:

> [For the sheep,] "The King will answer and say to them, 'Truly I say to you, to the extent that you did it to one of these brothers of Mine, even the least of them, you did it to Me.'" … [But for the goats,] "He will answer them, 'Truly I say to you, to the extent that you did not do it to one of the least of these, you did not do it to Me.'"[21]

Jesus made a radical connection between our dealings with the least and the last in the world and our dealings with God. Biblically this is not an aberrant remark. "One who is gracious to a poor man lends to the LORD," Proverbs says.[22]

In mysterious but unmistakable ways, God connected Himself to the suffering, the poor, and the least of these. The way we treat them is the way we treat Christ.

As individuals and as the American church, with whom are we confronted every day? Who is right in front of us on the road? From whom do we run away as fast as we can? Who are the people for whom we need to come down off our horses, kneel before in humility, and kiss their hands?

I was at a gas station in Los Angeles just after the devastating earthquakes hit Haiti, and I watched as a TV screen above the pump gave me a number to text in a ten-dollar donation. Everywhere I looked, celebrities and billboards provided opportunities to donate to this horrific human crisis. Giving in this form is often trendy, and it's wonderful to see.

But I've noticed that it's not yet fashionable to *touch* the untouchable.

Charity is pretty easy when it's a world away—when the only suffering we interact with is on websites and news reports. American Christians have found we can placate our consciences and satisfy a degree of missionary zeal by taking action about issues on the other side of the globe. We're always sending people "over there." We like doing mission this way because we don't have to get our hands dirty.

You and I are the missionaries who have been sent to the world in this time, country, and context. Somehow we need to discover the lepers right in front of us. Who wears the stigma? From whom are we turning away?

GET MESSY

To this day leprosy remains a real and tangible issue in our world; a recent study reports a quarter of a million cases globally.[23] Thankfully modern medicine can now treat the disease early on, so in nations where such medicine is available, the stigma is not as extreme. But in many third-world nations, leprosy remains a devastating disease, and it's only one of many infirmities that shipwreck lives into marginalization.

Countless situations exist today that mirror the plight of the ancient leper, and the church must bear the challenge of helping the modern leper—both overseas and in our own backyards.

In my own community, I look at our friends without homes and I see a stigmatized people. In many ways, they are the untouchables in Reality's backyard. As a result of studying the mission of Christ, many in our congregation began doing incredible things to reach out to them.

Some started a Laundry Love project, where they would wash the clothes of homeless people who couldn't afford it and then spend time with them at the Laundromat. Other members of our church started a program called Blanket Blessings and began taking blankets and warm clothes to help people without homes endure the rainy season in Southern California. Several folks lead a ministry in a local park, where we can share meals with the homeless. Some in our community don't just feed people—they eat *with* them.

Whenever we touch the untouchable, we risk consequences. Jesus knew the risks for a rabbi who touched a leper, and you and I will risk consequences as well.

At a recent Reality staff meeting, we discussed a new issue that surfaced at our Ventura campus: a number of people have come to church drunk. I'm not sure why this is happening, but we've dealt with this situation on numerous occasions. Our staff needed to discuss how to handle this issue and ultimately decide: Do we let drunk people come to church?

Very quickly we arrived at our conclusion.

Yes, we would welcome these people in. That's the way Jesus did ministry. The religious didn't like it, but Jesus spent time with the drunkards, the sinners, and the tax collectors. He touched the lepers!

Yes, we're absolutely going to allow drunken people to come into our church. Are there risks involved? Yes. It's a challenge for our staff and an issue of comfort and safety for others in attendance. Ultimately though, we believe these folks need to hear the gospel as much as the sober person sitting next to them, and we're going to do everything we can to see that happen.

Jesus shows us time and again that mission is going to get messy.

ARE WE WILLING?

You may have heard of Father Damien. He was a Belgian priest who, in the late nineteenth century, moved to the Hawaiian island of Molokai to minister to the leper colony there.

I've been to the island several times to go surfing and for various outreach trips, and once I stood on the hill overlooking the leper colony that still exists to this day.

Father Damien went to the most outcast and marginalized people he could find, and he ministered to them. After serving the lepers in Molokai for several years, he stood up one Sunday morning and opened his sermon with the words "We lepers are different."

He had contracted the disease.

Father Damien allowed himself to share in the sufferings of those he came to serve, to the degree that he was willing to die by the very same infirmity they bore.

The leper who met Jesus was untouchable, unclean, and yet somehow knew that Jesus would not be afraid or ashamed of associating with him. It wasn't normal, and it certainly wasn't fashionable, but Jesus' reputation was such that the leper believed he could come to Him.

Does the church represent that approachable Jesus today?

So many people—in our world, in our communities, and within our own church walls—feel like the leper in some way.

They feel rejected, outcast, and too sinful to be restored. They need to know that Jesus can cleanse every sin and heal every wound. Nothing has gone so wrong that our God cannot make it right, and all they must do is push through the crowd, fall down at His feet, and grab hold of Jesus.

Will we tell them?

The beauty of the Bible is that we see ourselves in each story. By way of analogy, each of us was a leper before we met Jesus. The power of God made our horrible, sinful lives beautiful, and it's my prayer that as we go out on mission, the stunning wonder of this miracle would not be lost on us.

Jesus had the power to make lepers clean—the leper never questioned that fact. The leper's question was whether or not Jesus was willing. You and I, because of the Spirit of God within us, have the power to do Christ's will in the world. We have the ability to do good and the opportunity to alleviate all kinds of suffering—physical and eternal.

The question for us today is not one of power or ability but of will.

Who are the people who feel outcast and untouchable in your immediate context? Who would Jesus have gone to? It could be your introverted coworker, an unpopular schoolmate, the elderly man on your street, an acquaintance who is disabled, or a neighbor with cancer. They may or may not have an obvious physical ailment, but if you pause to look for people who feel outcast, I promise you will find them.

When Jesus sought the lost and touched the untouchable, it changed the world. Missio Christi continues today, and each of us will be world changers to the degree that we are willing to partner with Christ in His mission.

Living at Godspeed means seeking out and going to the people Jesus would go to: the rejected, the marginalized, the poor, and the suffering. At times, our calling may take us to a remote region four continents away. But more often than not, our calling will take us somewhere much closer to home: downtown, across the street, to our local park, or right next-door.

The invitation for the Christian is woven throughout the New Testament.

"So then, while we have opportunity," says Galatians 6, "let us do good to all people."[24] Again in Hebrews, "Do not neglect doing good and sharing, for with such sacrifices God is pleased."[25]

The presupposition of the New Testament is that Christians have the ability, the anointing, and the occasion to do good, proclaim the gospel to those who need Jesus, and touch the untouchable in the world.

Are we willing?

7

FREE

Justice for the Guilty

The Gospel spreads best not through force, but through fascination.

Shane Claiborne

As a dad, I will never shake the memory of my little girl's first chemotherapy treatments.

Only weeks earlier Kate and I had received an urgent call from our daughter's elementary school: Daisy Love had fallen on the playground and was in and out of consciousness. Bodily scans at the hospital revealed a hemorrhaging tumor that covered nearly half of her abdominal cavity, and the doctors immediately diagnosed her with stage III cancer.

We were devastated.

After a storm of tests and hospital visits, we began my daughter's treatment with a team of trusted doctors. In this first month of chemo, we were still learning what to expect from Daisy's physical response.

That morning Daisy sat quietly as the nurse attached a unit of red chemo to her chest port. Kate and I leaned close and squeezed her tiny hands as the chemo drip began, bracing for the painful routine.

There was a long hush as the poison pumped into her chest.

Then in an instant Daisy's face swelled up and flushed red, and she vomited and peed as Kate and I shouted in panic. The nurse shut off the drip and rushed from the hospital room for help. In that single, horrific instant, I thought we were going to lose our daughter.

I laid hands over my limp little girl and prayed out loud, fervently.

A moment later doctors flooded the room, pumping her full of an antihistamine to counteract her reaction to the chemo. I held Daisy Love in my arms while her head, red and swollen, nodded back and forth as she lost consciousness. My mind swam as doctors hooked her to heavy machines, and we sat in silence as the green line beeped across the monitor. The nurses stayed to follow her vitals, waiting to see if she'd recover from the episode or need to be raced to the ICU.

We sat there for hours, Daisy Love curled in my arms.

It turned out that my five-year-old had been given an incorrect formulation of the chemo meant to kill her cancer. Not only that, but she was wrongly administered an adult dosage. To this day, Daisy still suffers psychological effects from her experience with the "red medicine," or what adult cancer patients refer to as "red death."

One week later Kate and I had an appointment to meet with the doctor responsible for that mistake. We were being advised to sue.

What does it mean to live out Missio Christi in that moment? When you are faced with the person responsible for an error that nearly took your daughter's life, how do you do mission?

JESUS AND THE ADULTEROUS WOMAN

Day broke over Jerusalem as Jesus entered the temple. It was the height of a Jewish religious festival, and the courtyard teemed with life. One by one, the crowd caught sight of the man who'd just arrived. Curious, they moved closer, eager to hear the words of the controversial carpenter from Nazareth.

Surrounded by people, Jesus sat down in the dust and began to teach.

It wasn't long before the religious leaders arrived. They pushed a downcast woman through the crowd and stopped her in front of Jesus.

Jesus stood up to meet her.

"Teacher," said the Pharisees with feigned respect, "this woman has been caught in adultery. In the very act."

Appealing to the Jewish audience around them, they continued, "In the law of Moses we are commanded to stone such women; what do you say?"

No matter how Jesus responded, they knew they'd have grounds to accuse Him. Satisfied, they waited for His response.

But Jesus didn't reply.

Instead He stooped down and began writing in the sand. Upset by His lack of a response, the Pharisees persisted—quoting the Jewish law and condemning the woman.

At last Jesus stood to face them and spoke.

"He who is without sin among you, let him be the first to throw a stone at her," He said. Then Jesus knelt to the ground once again, carving His message in the dust.

One by one, as the invitation settled in, the religious leaders moved away. The eldest departed first, followed by the youngest, until Jesus and the woman were left alone.

Jesus straightened up and said, "Woman, where are they? Does no one condemn you?"

Her accusers gone, she whispered, "No one, Lord."

Then Jesus spoke the words that free a broken life: "Neither do I condemn you. Go your way and from now on, sin no more."[1]

UNEXPECTED

The *Pericope Adulterae*, as scholars know this story, strikes a chord in almost all of us. The religious leaders' motives were unmistakable. Well acquainted with Jesus' message of mercy and compassion, of repentance and forgiveness, they brought a guilty woman before Him and quoted the law of Moses regarding punishment. If Jesus failed to uphold the law, they planned to condemn Him as a heretic and finally had the ammunition they needed to destroy His reputation as a rabbi.

Jesus' other option was to uphold the law and order the woman to be stoned. If He did this, He would have been arrested immediately. Under Roman rule, Israel could no longer perform capital punishment. A Jewish rabbi's execution order, consequently, would merit a criminal charge—a fact the religious leaders knew.

On top of this, the crowd watched. If Jesus allowed this woman's execution, what would it have communicated to His followers about His message of mercy and forgiveness?

Jesus had a dilemma. Whatever option He chose, He would lose to the Pharisees. But then the scene flipped and the woman's accusers shrank away in silent defeat.

Something about this story fascinates us. The adulterous woman was unmistakably guilty: she was caught in the act. The punishment for adultery was death by stoning, yet Jesus, who upheld the law perfectly at all times, set her free. He confounded every religious leader who accused her and sent her on her way with only a basic command: "*Sin no more.*"

The woman had just escaped execution—the lawful penalty for her actions—and this was the pep talk she got from God incarnate?

It's not the response we expect.

OUR MERIT MODEL

Culture influences Christianity. Naturally the way you and I practice Christianity today is affected by the society within which we live.

Twenty-first-century America is a merit-based culture. As a free society, we function on social and economic models of competition and strive to prove ourselves better than those around us. We are bred to compete and often judge one another almost exclusively on a value basis. There is no end to the ways Americans idolize and exalt high achievers; and on the other hand, there is no end to the ways we discount and dismiss poor performers.

The advent of social media and advance of technology in our daily lives only enhances the American economy of social competition. We openly share, rate, and compare—and the lack of face-to-face interaction eliminates direct relational consequences. We act more harshly online than we would ever dream of acting in person, especially to those we don't know. Our culture turns a girl into a pop star and treats her like a princess until she ends up in rehab or prison. Then we scoff at the pictures plastered in our supermarket line and choose another idol.

The American church today exists within this culture. The result is a valuation of people based upon their performances. The church makes up its own rules and rates people by them, both outside church walls as well as within. We rank sins to decide which are forgivable and which are not, and throw around terms like good Christian and bad Christian as though there is a difference between us in God's sight.

As American Christians, if we fail to form our identity in God's love for us, we will default to finding our identity by comparing ourselves to others. When we deploy these false moral and spiritual rating systems to credit and discredit the people around us, the result is a judgmental church.

OUR PLACE IN THE STORY

When we first read the story of the woman caught in adultery, we picture ourselves in the crowd—*as mere bystanders*. But when we consider our lives in light of sin and salvation, we see ourselves in the woman—*as sinners set free*.

Scripture tells us the wages of sin, any sin, is death.[2] We stand guilty before Jesus, who was without sin but bore its punishment on the cross to bring us redemption. Like this woman, we have experienced the extravagant kindness and undeserved mercy of Christ.

Most Christians get this. We are guilty but forgiven; we now live in freedom.

We like this math.

But it's a problem when we deal with other people.

Within the church, we have a tendency to care less about the person than we care about what he or she *did*. By this I mean that it's easy to recognize the sins of others, but rarely do we view sin in light of someone's personal need for mercy, love, and grace. Maybe this is why non-Christians in America view Christians as insensitive.[3]

When it comes to extending the mercy of Christ, we are often reluctant missionaries.

We look more like Jonah than Jesus.

Surely you heard the story of Jonah and the big fish when you were growing up. Do you remember how the fish swallowed the prophet Jonah when he didn't follow God's instruction and go to Nineveh? And do you remember *why* Jonah didn't go?

Jonah ran from God's call because he knew the Ninevites were radically wicked people, and he wanted them punished. This is made clear at the end of the book when Jonah complained to God. He essentially said, "God, I didn't want to go because I knew You were merciful and compassionate. I knew if I went and told them to repent of their sins, and they repented, that You would have had mercy on them."[4]

There is an irony to Jonah's rebellion.

This story demonstrates how Jonah, just like the Ninevites, was a sinner in need of God's forgiveness. Even after God rescued him from the consequence of his own sin, Jonah remained frustrated that God was compassionate and merciful to undeserving people. How often do we feel the same way?

The religious leaders in John 8 were in need of forgiveness themselves. At the very least, they were guilty of a double standard. They claimed to have caught the woman in the act of adultery,[5] which begs an obvious question: Where is the man? The Pharisees knew the law of Moses[6] demanded that both the woman *and* the man caught in adultery face the same consequence. By excusing one party while publicly condemning the other, the religious leaders violated the very law they claimed to uphold.

Like Jonah and the religious leaders, you and I are familiar with this double standard. We love mercy and grace when they are applied to our sins, deficiencies, and failures. But we get grace amnesia when it's time to deal with other people.

When someone commits a sin that threatens my comfort level, I have to fight my tendency to resort to judgment. I could just as easily become like the religious leaders and forget my own sins, condemn the other person, and fail to extend the very grace I've received.

The choice is ours.

If we're truly walking with Jesus, every day we will encounter individuals whose lives do not align with God's Word. Currently the world equates us with Pharisees, religious people known for condemning and judging. Our opportunity, however, is to act the way Jesus did.

IT'S ALL ABOUT RELATIONSHIP

In John 8, Jesus revealed God to be intensely relationship oriented rather than rule oriented. This should not surprise us. By definition, God *is* a relationship: Father, Son, and Holy Spirit.

Have you ever noticed how life is less fun when it's driven by rules? Maybe you go to church every week because those are the rules you've set: "Well, it's Sunday. I guess I have to go to church." That's not a mandate from God, and you don't satisfy Him when you go. It is a rule you've ordained for yourself, and you're probably not having fun.

Let me set you free: you don't need to be there. You're living a rule-oriented life.

Conversely if you go to church because you love Jesus, love His people, and love being in fellowship with them, Sunday attendance is not a rule—it's an opportunity. If this is the case, I'm certain your church experience is a joy.

What if your relationship with your spouse was rule oriented? Imagine if one party said to the other, "Here's the deal. On Monday you're going to do the dishes. Tuesday, the yard. Wednesday, you take out the trash. Thursday, we have sex, and Friday's our day off."

Can you imagine if those were the rules? How is that a joy?

"Honey, it's Thursday."

This example runs counter to the design of a healthy marriage. We wash dishes as an act of service. We do yardwork because we want to create a restful space to enjoy with our families. We make love because it's a relational gift ordained by God. Married or not, each of us desires a life driven by love and relationship, not rules.

A week after Daisy was given the wrong chemo, Kate and I met with the doctor responsible. I can hardly describe the emotions we experienced walking into his office. The news of our daughter's cancer had devastated us, and we'd already been overwhelmed by questions about what to do next, and in the midst of all this, someone administered to our daughter an adult formulation of the wrong chemotherapy—and it just about killed her.

As I mentioned before, we were being advised to sue.

This doctor's mistake was one of negligence, and not only his, there were others who failed that day, so by no means do I equate his actions with those of the guilty woman in John 8. My comparison, rather, is in the person and character of Jesus. He is the standard against which I measure *my* actions, even in the most devastating and disconcerting moments. His model unfailingly informs and enables each of us to live effectively on mission.

When Kate and I walked into that office, we wanted answers, we wanted accountability, and we wanted justice. But more than all those things, we wanted to look and act like Jesus.

And Jesus was kind to guilty people.

The doctor began our meeting somewhat nervous and defensive until we told him that we forgave him. We explained that we were Christians who'd been forgiven of much, and we wanted to extend the same forgiveness and grace to him and the cancer center.

Valuing relationship over rules in this circumstance changed everything for us. That doctor became the greatest advocate of Daisy's case and truly a beloved friend. Kate and I call him regularly for counsel and guidance, and his relationship has been invaluable through this difficult medical journey. He is still Daisy's oncologist today. In addition, the cancer center has blessed our family beyond measure in its ceaseless outpouring of love and concern for our daughter. And our church community has donated hundreds of stuffed animals for them to give to children suffering with cancer. It's a beautiful relationship.

One simple act—extending forgiveness and grace—allowed us to show Daisy's doctor the kindness of Christ, and it changed our experience with cancer treatment altogether.

PROPHETIC JUSTICE

Jesus values relationship over rules, and we see evidence of this in Scripture. But what this doesn't mean is that Jesus disregards the law or throws away the rules. He upheld the law perfectly and at all times.

In the story of John 8, Jesus challenged any religious leader without sin to throw the first stone.[7] He was willing to have the Mosaic law carried out to its full extent, but He set an impossible standard because something greater was at stake.

Is it always right for a strict and immediate application of the law and its consequences to take place? When it comes to others' sins, sometimes we want to say yes. I can think of plenty of times when I wanted to see justice paid out.

But does God handle us this way?

When we're envious of our neighbor's new car, lie about why we were late, or speak rudely to the Starbucks barista because she made our drink wrong, God does not mete out immediate justice on us. There are human consequences for our actions (the barista might not greet us warmly at Starbucks next time), but we're spared immediate divine judgment for our sinful actions.

In the prophecies of Isaiah, a section called the "Servant Songs" characterizes Jesus the Messiah as a suffering servant. Isaiah 42:3 says, "A bruised reed He will not break, and a dimly burning wick He will not extinguish; He will faithfully bring forth justice."

Jesus cares about justice, but He also cares about people in anguish. Jesus did not come to break the bruised reed, the person deeply wounded by the consequences of sin. He did not come to snuff out the dimly burning wick, the person barely hanging on to the flicker of hope they have left.

Jesus cares infinitely for broken sinners. Isaiah tells us that He will faithfully bring forth justice; but catch the word *will*—it's in the future tense. There is a prophetic element to the justice of God—and this allows His compassion to be exercised now.

The religious leaders in John 8 wanted strict and immediate application of the law. Jesus, on the other hand, chose compassion for the woman before Him. A woman bruised by her sin, a woman whose hope was dwindling.

Jesus was and is on a mission of mercy to set sinners free. He declared this publicly in Luke 4:18–19: "He has sent Me to proclaim release to the captives, and recovery of sight to the blind, to set free those who are oppressed, to proclaim the favorable year of the Lord."

But Jesus communicated something staggering by what He *didn't* say. He cut the passage short and rolled up the scroll.[8]

The second half of the sentence—preserved for us in Isaiah 61:2—finishes this way: "and the day of vengeance of our God." Jesus' Jewish audience knew this scripture well, and they knew the words that came next.

It would be as if I told you, "Jack and Jill went up the hill"—then stopped. You would know the reason was to fetch a pail of water because you know the nursery rhyme. You would understand that I communicated something purposeful by stopping where I did. Jesus' audience understood that here as well.

After reading Isaiah's prophecy, Jesus told His listeners that it had been fulfilled in their hearing.[9] Jesus' life on earth was the fulfillment of only the first half of the prophecy: the coming of the kingdom of God and, along with it, God's favor and kindness.

The day of vengeance, or judgment, that the book of Isaiah speaks of is yet to come.

Knowing this final judgment is ahead helps us process the horrific injustices we see across the globe today: abuse, poverty, human trafficking, and genocide. One day Jesus will return to right every wrong and judge every evil known to humankind.

Today we work for present justice in every government, relationship, and circumstance we can, all the while understanding that perfect justice has not yet arrived. But we weren't sent to judge the world. That's Christ's job when He returns.

The church joins Christ on mission, and yet we've gotten ahead of Jesus. We take it upon ourselves to judge the actions of others (as we discussed in chapter 3), even though Jesus Himself declared this to be the age of God's favor and grace. According to the book of Romans, the Holy Spirit draws men and women to repentance and does so by revealing the kindness of God.[10] When we show Christ's kindness to people, we partner with the Holy Spirit in leading them to repentance.

This is what made the shift with Daisy's doctor so beautiful: we participated in showing him the kindness of Christ.

TRUTH WITHOUT COMPROMISE

After Jesus freed the woman from condemnation, He told her to sin no more. It sounds like He actually thought it was going to work too: "I don't condemn you. You're free. And by the way, don't sin anymore."[11]

Unlike Jesus, we have a difficult time letting people off the hook and pointing them to grace. We instinctively believe that unless rules are applied hard and fast, no one will obey or fear God. And this is probably true … for two-year-olds.

But not for the rest of humanity.

Today we see a migration of disenfranchised people leaving the church. At some point along the way, we (the church) hurt them. We grew more concerned with applying rules and consequences. We lacked compassion and a prophetic view of justice.

If we heard their stories, we'd learn they come from wounded places.

One such person is Serena Woods. Serena was born to a fifteen-year-old mom and abused as a child. She grew up in foster care and became a single mother at age nineteen. Serena accepted Christ while she was pregnant. Afterward she married, became a mother of three, and got actively involved in the church. Then she had an affair with her best friend's husband, and her world fell apart:

> There is no price I could pay that would take away the damage I did. The crimes stacked upon crimes crushed me. The people who I hurt were lined up so far in the distance that eventually I didn't even know who they were.... When Jesus found me, I was inside-out with grief. I couldn't pay up. My value disappeared and my debt remained. Jesus pointed to the day on the calendar where his body opened up and spilled his life.... And Jesus said, "What I did is bigger than this. Your sin is what that was for."[12]

In the story in John 8, Jesus spoke to the religious leaders just once, saying, "He who is without sin among you, let him be the first to throw a stone at her."[13]

At first this looks like a holy gimmick—as if Jesus was setting up the Pharisees to embarrass them. But God's Word is infallible. Jesus meant what He said.

He was willing to allow any person who was not a sinner deserving of death to carry out the full punishment for this woman's adultery. The law demanded it, and Jesus upheld the law perfectly. The religious leaders move away because not one of them was free from sin. Every person present was a sinner.

Every person, that is, except Jesus. He was the only One worthy to carry out the penalty the woman's iniquity deserved because He was the only One without sin. And the punishment of death must be carried out.

But rather than place it on her, Jesus would bear it Himself on the cross.

Because of what happened at Calvary, we never have to compromise God's truths to be compassionate. Some in the church will argue that the meaning of the Bible changes with culture. They will dismiss the authority and inerrancy of the timeless Word of God in the name of practicing compassion. But Jesus never compromised truth in order to practice compassion. In John 8, He fully upheld the sexual code of the Old Testament.

Yet here's the amazing thing: while upholding the law perfectly, *Jesus removed the penalty.*

The modern church believes that if we don't punish people for their sins, they will never return to obedience. So we punish them, and then they never return to church. That's not to say we shouldn't practice church discipline; we should. But not church punishment. The grace of Christ is without pretense. Jesus bore the cost, and we get to extend grace on His behalf.

Serena lost her entire Christian community as a result of her affair. Rather than help restore her, the people in her church condemned her. She didn't need her church to reinforce how terrible her sin was; her life was utterly destroyed by it.

Only through the grace of Jesus Christ has she since been renewed, set free, and able to forgive the community that abandoned her. Today Serena makes it her mission to share about the undeserved grace of God with anyone who will listen and everyone who needs it:

> I was once told, *"I don't know how God can redeem this and scrape together what could remain of your life to glorify Him."* Well, I'm starting to see a picture of that now. I don't know if I'll ever be able to see all that God is doing with His painting of me, but what little I *can* catch a glimpse of sends me straight to His feet in worship.[14]

Psalm 130:3–4 says, "If You, LORD, should mark iniquities … who could stand? But there is forgiveness with You, that You may be feared." God works in humanity in such a way that His kindness draws us to repentance.

Effective ministry often comes through the most broken people, for their poverty makes them acutely aware of the limitless riches of Jesus' grace.

"Don't you see how wonderfully kind, tolerant, and patient God is with you?" asks Romans 2:4. "Does this mean nothing to you? Can't you see that his kindness is intended to turn you from your sin?"

God's kindness turns us from our sin and turns us toward Him. As followers of Christ, we are to embody that same kindness.

Imagine what the future of the American church would look like if we rose up a generation of theologically sound leaders known for their grace and compassion. Imagine how culture would respond if the church offered a kinder orthodoxy.

The church would welcome people more, hurt one another less, and ultimately look more like Jesus. Just think what the statistics would say then!

THROUGH FASCINATION

If I were in Jesus' place in John 8, I think I would have—like He did—told the woman caught in adultery not to sin anymore. I would have emphasized the immense gravity of her actions, made certain that she and the crowd understood, and then asked her to promise never to do it again. After I was really sure she got it, maybe then I would let her off the hook.

Unlike me, Jesus set this woman free *before* He told her not to sin anymore. He reversed the order! His method sounds completely backward, but this is the gospel message. Not "You better do ..." but "Look what Jesus has done!" Freedom from sin's consequence comes first, then obedience follows.

Imagine how fascinating it must have been for the woman and that crowd of onlookers. She was guilty yet completely set free. The heart of this story, we realize, is not about a woman who got off the hook for her sin. It's really about Jesus, who put Himself on the hook in her stead. Jesus canceled the charge against her because He would take her sin to the cross with three nails in her place.[15]

Condemnation and judgment do not win people to Jesus, but fascination does. Grace we don't deserve, kindness we don't expect, and the sacrificial love of a Savior willing to die in our place fascinates us.

As you and I endeavor to extend grace and exhibit authentic kindness toward people, we must remember that these flow from the active working of the Holy Spirit in our lives. Grace and kindness are the result of God's transforming power in us, they are not the results of our own goodness. This truth removes the pressure for the Christian to perform but reinforces the need for us to know Jesus more.

First John 2:5–6 says, "By this we know that we are in Him: the one who says he abides in Him ought himself to walk in the same manner as He walked."

We need more of Jesus in our lives; we need a deeper relationship with Him in order to engage people as He did. At the same time, when we fully abide in Jesus, our lives will look similar to His. Jesus' work will be evident in us as His mission begins to manifest through us.

Remember the good news: Jesus offers salvation to all of humanity. When we see people in light of this truth, this insight alters the way we deal with the sins of others. Instead of judging and condemning like the Pharisees did, we can capture the opportunity to demonstrate the person and character of Christ.

When we treat people like Jesus treated people, the Holy Spirit works to draw them to repentance and set them free from sin. But they aren't the only ones: you and I are set free from sinfully taking God's rightful place as judge. We can look back to the cross, where God's judgment and justice were met, and forward to the second coming of Christ, where His judgment and justice will be dealt.

When we do that, we can then extend genuine kindness and extravagant grace to people who (like us!) do not deserve it.

"It was for freedom that Christ set us free," Galatians 5:1 says.

God set us free from sin that we might partner with Jesus to bring His freedom to others. Herein lies Missio Christi.

Mission will counter culture and fascinate our friends, because the church will look like Jesus in the world.

8

RESTORE

Generosity for the Greedy

Love interrupts … the consequences of our actions.

Bono

"You're looking kinda old, dude."

Ouch.

The Facebook comment under my new profile picture was from a guy I grew up with. Maybe I *am* looking more grown-up these days (Kate said she likes the photo), but that doesn't matter. His next comment stung:

"You were such a **** to me in high school. All's good now. What would Jesus think?!"

This line cut deep.

Most days I hardly remember the person I was back in high school. He feels eons away, until moments like these that jog my memory. It amazes me that I hurt a person to the degree that he would post about it on Facebook two decades later.

"That is one of the reasons I needed Jesus …" I posted in my reply.

There was no deleting the past, so all I could do was confess the sin, exalt the person of Christ who redeemed me, and apologize in front of all my "friends."

"I am sorry about high school and how I treated you … I wish I could do it over again … I was a different person then." The statement couldn't be truer. I was mean to people in those days: Christians and non-Christians alike.

Tyler, one of my best friends today and an elder at Reality, remembers attending high school with me. When he met with the Christian Club on campus each week, my buddies and I would chuck milk cartons at them from across the quad.

Full milk cartons.

I accepted Jesus as a little kid, but by the time I hit high school, I laughed at the Christians and called them derogatory names. I wouldn't associate with "Bible thumpers" and had no problem marginalizing them and anyone else I found less than cool.

How shocking that God would choose someone like me, of all people, to teach His Word and to pastor His church in the same town!

One of the most noteworthy changes in the twenty-first-century church is our radical shift toward issues of social justice. We demonstrate the person of Jesus by caring for those in greatest need: orphans, AIDS victims, trafficking survivors, and the impoverished. We've only scratched the surface when it comes to meeting their needs, but socially we've helped make it popular and commendable—*even expected*—to turn our time and our attention toward the "least of these."[1]

We want relief for the poor and justice for the oppressed. This is right and this is beautiful and this is biblical.

But what do we want for the oppressors?

What do we want for the guys who hurl milk cartons?

JESUS AND THE TAX COLLECTOR

Rumors of Jesus' coming flew around the city. As Jesus and the disciples entered Jericho, a parade of fascinated people joined them.

Among those in the crowd was a Jewish man named Zacchaeus. Arguably one of the most powerful men in Jericho, Zacchaeus was the chief tax collector of the city.

He was also—unfortunately for him on this day—exceedingly short in stature. Unable to glimpse Jesus through the horde of onlookers, Zacchaeus sprinted far ahead and fumbled his way up a sycamore tree. There he waited, perched in the branches like a ten-year-old boy.

Soon the parade of people reached his tree. Craning his neck, Zacchaeus finally saw the face of Jesus of Nazareth.

Then, with a start, Zacchaeus realized Jesus had stopped beneath the sycamore and looked straight up at him. The throng of people following Jesus also paused to gaze upward, gawking at the tax collector.

"Zacchaeus, hurry and come down," Jesus called. "For today I must stay at your house."

Branches creaked and leaves filtered down as Zacchaeus tumbled from the tree to where Jesus waited. Unable to contain his joy, Zacchaeus received Jesus and led Him warmly to his home.

All evening people talked about it.

"He has gone to be the guest of a man who is a sinner." The denigration echoed throughout Jericho, but Zacchaeus neither heard nor cared. Jesus, the Son of God, was dining in his home!

The meal ended; the time for pretense had past. Zacchaeus stood. "Behold, Lord, half of my possessions I will give to the poor," he said. "And if I have defrauded anyone of anything, I will give back four times as much."

The wealthy tax collector meant every word.

Jesus turned at this pronouncement and looked Zacchaeus square in the eyes. "Today salvation has come to this house," the Messiah declared before His disciples, "because he, too, is a son of Abraham."[2]

BOTH ENDS OF THE SPECTRUM

The mission of Christ surprises humanity.

The Gospels thrust the "least of these" before us, because these are the people always before Jesus. Our calling to care for them is clear. Again and again Jesus went to the meek, the poor, the powerless, and the oppressed—and they were the ones He called blessed.[3]

But Zacchaeus was none of these.

According to Luke, Zacchaeus was no ordinary tax collector—he was a *chief* tax collector.

In Jesus' day, Rome recruited Jewish nationals to collect state taxes. They required a certain amount of collection, and whatever a tax collector gathered in excess he kept as his profit. The more Zacchaeus took advantage of his fellow Jews, the wealthier he became. If anyone protested his math or methodologies, Zacchaeus had the backing of Roman centurions to enforce his extortion.

Throughout the New Testament, we see the terms *tax collector* and *sinner* lumped together in the same category. In a very religious society like this, people considered tax collectors among the most irreligious. Yet when Jesus entered Jericho, He called out only one person by name: Zacchaeus, a man who embodied the object of the community's hatred.

The chapter preceding this one, Luke 18, depicted a scene that took place just minutes prior. Jesus was on His way into the city when a blind man cried out from the side of the road.

"Jesus, Son of David, have mercy on me!" Hearing him, Jesus stopped and asked for the man to be brought over.

"What do you want Me to do for you?" Jesus asked.

The man's request was simple. "Lord," he said, "I want to regain my sight."

And Jesus responded, "Receive your sight; your faith has made you well."

Luke tells us the blind man got what he asked for immediately. It was a miraculous restoration. The people watched in awe and praised God. The once-blind man joined them, praising God as well.[4]

That miraculous healing was still on everyone's mind when Jesus stopped beneath Zacchaeus's tree.

The blind man called out to Jesus from the side of the road; minutes later Jesus called out to an oppressor. The juxtaposition of these two stories is striking.

We see that Jesus not only loves the victims of suffering and injustice, but He also loves the perpetrators of those very injustices. Jesus pursues *both* the oppressed and the oppressor in mission.

The story of Zacchaeus reveals a compassionate Messiah who is concerned about the people at both ends of the spectrum of injustice. This fact stunned the crowd of Jericho then, and it makes the church uncomfortable today.

CARRY-ON BAGGAGE

In *Jesus Through Middle Eastern Eyes*, Kenneth Bailey gave an enhanced historical context of the Luke 19 narrative. According to Bailey, the appropriate (and expected) response from Jesus would have gone like this:

> Zacchaeus, you are a collaborator! You are an *oppressor* of these good people. You have drained the economic lifeblood of your people and given it to the imperialists. You have betrayed your country and your God. This community's hatred of you is fully justified. You must quit your job, repent, journey to Jerusalem for ceremonial purification, return to Jericho and apply yourself to keeping the law. If you're willing to do these things, on my next trip to Jericho I will enter your newly purified house and offer my congratulations.

Bailey continued, "Such a speech would have provoked long and enthusiastic applause."[5] Certainly the religious Jews of Jesus' day wanted people to change, but they wanted to see repentance before the person would be welcomed back.

The church today operates in a similar way.

As Christians, we want to see people change and make retribution. But often we ask them to do this *before* they enter our community. First, we want to see the unjust, the powerful, and the oppressors get busted. We hope wayward sinners will deal with their issues and turn their lives around before they sit next to us in church. Rarely do we open the door and offer love, grace, mercy, and acceptance first.

There are people outside our church walls who want to come in and meet Jesus. We wave them in, inviting them to wipe their feet on an entry mat that reads "Welcome—You Can Come in Once You Get a Few Things Fixed."

The people who need Christian community most are precisely those whose lives are *not* in order. They know our expectations. They also know their own deficiencies. And so they hightail it for the hills.

Now maybe I've been traveling too much lately, but I think the church has become a lot like America's religious TSA. We screen all their baggage. Oh, carry-on baggage we're okay with. After all, everyone has one or maybe two small items. Larger baggage we can handle too, but we like to put it out of sight as quickly as possible—and the heavier the bag, the higher the fee.

Airport security has nothing on church background checks.

We poke and prod at people's personal history, examining testimonies for anything suspicious or irregular. The more closely a church visitor fits our standard, the quicker he or she will get in the door. Body piercings set off our detectors, citizens who look Middle Eastern go straight off to interrogation, and for the teen who packs a firecracker—well, we all know he won't be flying anytime soon.

As members of the church, we establish unspoken "rules" because we don't know how to deal with the issues, vices, and bad habits—*the baggage*—people bring with them. Anything that might get messy needs to be sealed away in a Ziploc bag. To make "Churchianity" easy, we prefer to confiscate and quarantine these things.

As followers of Jesus, you and I desire to see sinners brought to repentance. We genuinely want to help them change and transform. But we falter by making change a *prerequisite* for entry into community. By requiring broken people to conform to our "rules" before they are allowed to belong, we throw up barriers to the work of Jesus in their lives.

THE NEEDS OF THE WORLD (REDEFINED)

Recently, during the worst economic climate since the Great Depression, Americans gave more than three hundred billion dollars to nonprofit organizations.[6]

What a beautiful picture.

Now more than ever, compassion is in fashion. Charity is a part of our cultural DNA, both inside and outside the church. Over the last half century, benevolent giving in America has grown faster than the American economy,[7] and today our country is home to more than one million nonprofits.[8]

Amid this climate of giving, the modern church has mounted a social and cultural revolution around issues of mercy and justice. This is especially important because extending care to those in great need paints a picture of Jesus.

But our benevolence has limits.

While we care for the "least of these," we often expect and desire divine judgment for people who have abused wealth and power to exploit others. We would like to see harsh justice inflicted on the perpetrators of oppression. Ironically we consider the oppressors "unreachable" by God's grace, and ultimately we condemn them.

Which brings us back to the subject of judgment.

As we work for justice, we must remember that God did not commission us to judge the world—not even those who seem most deserving. When we render people unforgivable, we underestimate and misinterpret the extravagant grace of God in Christ.

Ephesians 6 reminds us that our battle is not against flesh and blood. So whatever evils these oppressors employ, our *true* war is against the powers and principalities of darkness that perpetuate systems of injustice.

Recently I heard a story about a pastor in Korea who led his congregation in a dedicated time of prayer for the issue of human trafficking. The church prayed fervently for the victims of this horrific crime, but they didn't stop there. The congregation went on to pray for the customers who created the demand and for the traffickers who filled it. They interceded, asking for slaves to be set free and for oppressors to be released from the bonds of lust, greed, and sin. When the congregation pleaded for God to "set the captives free," they interceded for the slaves, traffickers, and customers alike.

The American church is learning to see and meet the needs of the poor and oppressed. But if all we do is perform acts of charity, how are we different from other benevolent Americans? By reaching *both* the oppressed and the oppressors, the mission of Christ redefines the needs of the world.

The New Testament highlights one oppressor uniquely: a persecutor named Saul, whom you and I know as the apostle Paul.

When Jesus met him on the road to Damascus, Saul was a Pharisee, a murderer, and a violent persecutor of the young Christian faith. The early church would've known few greater tyrants. Yet this oppressor was the very man Jesus chose to pastor His people and communicate His gospel—the message we read in our Bibles today.

Paul's example offers a vivid portrait of how Jesus not only reaches out to oppressors in mission but also how He often uses their renewal to further the work of His kingdom.

In the book of Mark, we see Jesus and the disciples dining with yet another tax collector named Levi and a group of other "disreputable sinners." As usual, word gets back to the Pharisees, who demand to know why a rabbi ate with such "scum."

Jesus' response to their accusation was succinct.

"Healthy people don't need a doctor—sick people do," He said. "I have come to call not those who think they are righteous, but those who know they are sinners."[9] Time and again, Jesus sought out and spent time with the spiritually sick and the morally bankrupt.

Are these the same people Jesus is leading you to reach?

INVITATION OVER

In the Gospels, Jesus never required people to change before He demonstrated His love toward them.

The church today gets this backward. Often. We expect people's transformation before we invite them into participation.

The love of Christ pursues, and Zacchaeus experienced this firsthand. That day on the dusty streets of Jericho, Jesus ignored the religious crowds around Him and went straight to the object of their hatred, the human representation of their oppression: imperialistic Rome. Despised collaborator, traitor to both nation and religion—*that's* what Jewish tax collectors were.

Notice that on that day in Jericho, Jesus didn't invite Zacchaeus to come along with the group, nor did He suggest meeting up later. Jesus let the tax collector *lead*. He suggested going to the place where Zacchaeus felt comfortable, where Zacchaeus could offer something of value. As with the woman at the well, Jesus reached a broken person by putting Himself in need.

What Jesus did was not customary, as the culture of the day was based on the concept of dignity. A Jewish traveler would never dishonor himself by inviting himself over to a stranger's home.[10] Today's culture isn't so different. It isn't socially acceptable to invite yourself over to someone else's house for dinner. We simply do not do this.

At least most of us don't. I may be an exception.

One of our pastors at Reality, Todd, is married to a wonderful woman named Trista who could be America's next top chef. Their house is beautiful and comfortable and spotless (they don't have any kids, clearly!). Kate and I love spending time in their home.

Recently Todd and Trista invited our new church planter, Al, and his wife, Nina, over for a meal. I was with Al earlier that week when he casually mentioned the dinner.

"Great!" I exclaimed. "Kate and I will come too."

Al immediately broke into damage control mode. "Uh … well, how about I call them first, Britt? Let me check and make sure that's okay."

You see, Al is new in town. He didn't know that I invite myself over to people's houses regularly.

Later that day Al called Trista to try to explain that I'd included my wife and me in their invitation. Sweet Trista, of course, knew the routine.

"Yes, Britt always does that. Bring them over. That will be perfect."

People who know me well understand that behind my self-inviting is authentic love. Kate and I have genuine love for Todd and Trista, which they reciprocate. By inviting myself over, I stake a claim in our solid foundation of friendship.

The logic was the same in Jesus' day. When an orthodox Jew said, "I want to have supper with you," it meant, "I want to enter into friendship with you."

Zacchaeus's community merely tolerated him, isolating him from the rest of the neighborhood. Jesus, on the other hand, saw Zacchaeus as he was and believed in who he could become and, therefore, invited Himself to dinner.[11]

Jesus' friendship with sinners gave the world a tangible picture of the grace of God.[12] This pursuing love is the precursor to changing a person's life.

And it's also the catalyst.

COUNTERFEITS

The book of Luke speaks to issues of poverty and injustice, but it also draws our attention to the other problem: power and affluence. Throughout Luke's gospel, status and wealth are displayed as significant hindrances to true and thriving discipleship.[13] Jesus, in fact, presented money as the single most challenging counterfeit to the one true God.

Issues of poverty are tragic physically, and issues of idolatry are tragic spiritually. "No one can serve two masters," Jesus said in Luke 16. "For you will hate one and love the other; you will be devoted to one and despise the other. You cannot serve both God and money."[14]

It was the love of money that led Zacchaeus to become an oppressor and exploiter of his fellow men. By the time Jesus came to town, the tax collector's all-consuming love for the idol of wealth had lured him deep into sin.

Humanity was created in God's image for His glory; His glory is our purpose for being. When sin first entered the picture at Eden, it distorted that purpose. The image of God within us became muddied, marred, and perverted.

Enter the Messiah.

By Jesus' death and resurrection, you and I are new creatures. The image of God is restored in us; we are redeemed image bearers.

Yet whenever we exalt something to the place of supremacy in our lives, we distort the image of the true God within us. When we follow after lesser things, these counterfeit gods, it inhibits our ability to rightly bear God's image.

From Genesis to Revelation, the Bible sings of the nature of God as a generous giver. He doesn't manipulate us to coax a response nor invest in us that He might earn a profit. God is pure giver. He gives out of His character and generously so to those of us who don't deserve it.

You and I were created in the image of this generous God. When we fall in love with idols, we misdirect our worship and become greedy takers instead of the generous givers God intended.

Which is right where Zacchaeus was when Jesus met him.

JESUS MATH

I know a woman named Cheryl who always has a difficult time accepting gifts. One night she and her husband went out to dinner with friends, and when the check arrived, the other couple reached to grab it.

The typical banter ensued—"Let us get it!" "No, we insist!"—until suddenly the other couple grew serious.

"Please just accept graciously," they said. Needless to say, Cheryl and her husband got a free meal that night.

Since then, Cheryl frequently has used the phrase herself. Anytime she wants to buy someone a gift, treat a friend to coffee, or cover the tab at lunch, she says, "Please accept graciously," and it works like a charm.

Who doesn't want to accept a gift graciously?

This is what we get to do with Jesus. We accept His gift graciously because there's no way we could ever repay it.

Humans have always wondered: What must a person *do* to win favor with God? This question begs other questions, such as How good are a person's good deeds? and Will all those good deeds tip the scale? This question is at the core of every major world religion.

But Jesus invents a new arithmetic. In Luke 19:10, Jesus explained His mission: "For the Son of Man has come to seek and to save that which was lost."

Second Peter 3:9 says the Lord "is patient toward you, not wishing for any to perish but for all to come to repentance."

The free gift of salvation through Christ defies all logic. It is unearned and unmerited, but we must turn from our sin and repent to receive it. "As many as received Him," says John 1:12, "to them He gave the right to become children of God."

Zacchaeus's example is one of gracious acceptance. Luke 19:6 reveals that he gladly received Jesus, and his life was transformed.

"Behold, Lord," Zacchaeus said, "half of my possessions I will give to the poor, and if I have defrauded anyone of anything"—and we know he had—"I will give back four times as much."

To "restore" something means to return it to its correct condition. In his greed and oppression of others, Zacchaeus had become less than God created him to be. Jesus was looking to set this man aright, to restore him so he might live generously.

What we see in the tax collector is the Holy Spirit's radical restoration. A life set on fire to live at Godspeed.

Zacchaeus would give away half of everything he owned. He would go back to every person he had ever extorted and repay each person four times the amount originally taken. The Old Testament books of Leviticus and Numbers spell out the law's requirement for making restitution, and what Zacchaeus was offering was 300 percent more!

Zacchaeus was not operating by the law. He was operating by his experience of grace.

Because of Jesus' unlikely pursuit of him, Zacchaeus took a journey from greed to generosity, from self-centeredness to sacrifice. Where he had once oppressed the poor, Zacchaeus now championed justice. Where he had accrued wealth at the cost of others, he now served others at his own expense.[15]

Zacchaeus experienced authentic restoration. "Today salvation has come to this house," Jesus said.[16] The response is remarkable, but it's the timing of this process that's key.

Zacchaeus's restoration happened *after* Jesus went to be with him, not before. Zacchaeus didn't make his proclamation from the tree, saying, "Jesus, I will repay those I've robbed … if you restore me." Jesus' favor was unmerited. Jesus chose to dine in Zacchaeus's home precisely because the tax collector was unworthy and in need.

Only after experiencing time with Christ do we see Zacchaeus change. His proclamation of repayment was the outflow of his transformation and restoration.

Laws and rules and religion couldn't change him. Peer pressure and scorn from his community did not sway him. The element that transformed the crooked life of this small, exploitative tax collector was the hospitality of grace. It was kindness that led him to repentance.[17] Once more, relationship was both the context and the conduit for ministry.

Missio Christi leads us to spend time with the types of people Jesus spent time with. It compels us to befriend the mean-spirited and the marginalizing, because the kindness of Christ—*manifested through us*—points oppressors to grace.

YOU'RE ATTRACTIVE

Have you ever noticed that we look like what we love? It practically leaks from our pores. I can think of best friends I know who dress alike and newlywed couples who mimic each other's mannerisms.

Not only do we do this with people, but we also do it with things. I love surfing, and I can't help that I look like a surfer. I see people walking down the street with their dogs, and often they actually look like their dogs! I know success mongers, and their hunger for opportunity is palpable in the air around them. I know people who chase celebrity and people who love their money. These obsessions drive the courses of their lives, and you can feel it when you spend time with them.

Consuming adoration both absorbs and reflects its object, and this is great news for the Christian—if what we love most is Jesus.

As we participate in Missio Christi, the greatest hindrance to our ministry will be the moment we put a lesser god in the place of supremacy in our lives. This is why Jesus warned so specifically against it.

Is there anything—or *anyone*—you love more than Jesus?

This is the question I asked myself when Kate and I first learned of Daisy Love's cancer. The night before her first operation, I had no idea if she was going to live or die. It was my own dark night of the soul. As I prayed on the floor, I remembered other nights—better nights—when I would kiss sweet Daisy's face and tuck her under the covers and tell her I loved her more than anything else in the world.

"Nuh-uh, Daddy!" she always said. "Not more than Jesus!"

As I pleaded and interceded for my little girl's life that night, I knew I had to anchor my faith in exactly what she'd always told me.

"Jesus," I prayed, "whatever happens tomorrow, nothing changes between You and me. If I lose my little girl, I will still love You more than everything else."

Faith and mission always return to the simple bedrock of loving Jesus most. And when we love Jesus most, we will look more like Him.

Jesus didn't force Himself upon Zacchaeus. He didn't go to Zacchaeus's home and knock on the door and ask to be invited in. Jesus attracted Zacchaeus to Himself. Jesus fascinated the oppressor—enough to make him climb a tree just to catch a glimpse of the Jesus he had heard about. It was underneath a sycamore that Jesus called out to Zacchaeus and scandalously invited Himself into friendship.

Jesus came to meet the needs of the world, and He attracted the needy to Himself. He attracted the poverty-stricken and the wealthy, the oppressed and the oppressor: all of whom were in desperate need spiritually.

I was not impoverished physically when Jesus met me, but I was impoverished spiritually. I marginalized people I didn't like. People like my Facebook friend are scarred to this day because of the way I treated them. Jesus met me in my need, and the Holy Spirit used specific people around me—people already walking with Jesus on mission—to draw me to repentance.

As we love others and look more like Jesus, we attract the same kinds of people He attracted—people like Zacchaeus and people like me in high school. We can then show the mean, the unjust, and the oppressors the same kindness we show to the poor, the hurt, and the oppressed.

This is the kindness that draws souls to repentance.

And by it we will see the lives of people at both ends of injustice restored.

PART 3

THE SPIRIT'S MINISTRY THROUGH MISSIO CHRISTI

"… I also send you."

9

RENEW

God's Process for All Things

The task of every generation is to discover in which direction the Sovereign Redeemer is moving, then move in that direction.

Jonathan Edwards

A family in our church was recently driving down the road in town. They crossed an overpass above the 101 freeway and saw a young man sitting on the curb.

As they drove past, the father turned to his family. "Something wasn't right about that kid," he said. "Something was off. Maybe we should—"

Before he could finish, his daughter chimed in: "Yeah, Dad, something was wrong. I think the Spirit's telling us to do something. Let's go back."

The family hung a U-turn and pulled up next to the teenage boy.

"Hey," the father said, "are you okay?"

"No," the young man replied, "I was about to kill myself."

The teen went on, "I've been sitting on this bridge getting ready to jump off. I was hoping that someone would notice. I counted seventy-eight cars go by, and no one noticed me … but you stopped. If you didn't, I was going to jump."

Because this family heard the Spirit and obeyed, they prevented the loss of a precious life that day.

What is the difference between doing mission our way and doing mission God's way? What is at stake when it comes to following the Holy Spirit's lead?

Everything.

JESUS AND THE GERASENE DEMONIAC

Jesus and the disciples crossed the Sea of Galilee and entered the country of the Gerasenes. As Jesus climbed out of the boat, a man ran toward Him.

An unclean spirit possessed the man, who had been living in the nearby tombs. Night and day he had cried out in the mountains and scraped his body with stones. He'd been bound repeatedly with shackles and chains; each time he had torn them to pieces. No man was strong enough to subdue him.

The demoniac saw the boat approach from a distance. Running forward, He fell at Jesus' feet and cried out, "What do you want with me, Jesus, Son of the Most High God?"

"Come out of the man, you unclean spirit!" Jesus commanded.

"I implore You by God, do not torture me!" he cried.

"What is your name?" Jesus asked.

"My name is Legion," the man said. "For we are many."

And they pleaded with Jesus not to send them out of the country. A large herd of pigs fed nearby on the side of the mountain. "Send us into the swine," the demons begged, "let us go into them."

Jesus gave permission. The unclean spirits left the man and entered the swine, about two thousand of them. And as they did, the pigs rushed down the ragged bank to the water and drowned in the sea. Seeing this, the herdsmen ran away and reported it in the city and countryside. People came from all around to witness the scene.

They saw the man, once possessed by a legion of demons, now sitting down, clothed, and in his right mind. Those who'd seen the event described what had happened in fear, and they pleaded with Jesus, asking Him to leave the area.

As Jesus and the disciples got back into the boat, the Gerasene man ran toward them and asked if he could come with them.

Instead, Jesus said, "Go home to your people and report to them what great things the Lord has done for you, and how He had mercy on you."

The man went to Decapolis and proclaimed the great things Jesus had done. And everyone marveled.[1]

INTENTIONALITY

When Kate and I wake up to a sunny Saturday morning, we often call our friends and plan a time to meet at the beach. We're intentional as we pack to leave, because when it comes to the Merrick family, we have a ton of beach stuff.

Each of the kids brings a boogie board and a skim board. Isaiah has a surfboard, Kate has a surfboard, and I have a surfboard. And then I need an extra surfboard. Just in case. On top of that, there are two umbrellas, five towels, four lunches, three beach chairs, two coolers (and a partridge in a pear tree).

Going to the beach is our family's favorite way to spend a day, and we intentionally bring everything we need for a fun-filled afternoon. When it comes to family recreation, we're incredibly intentional.

Most people are intentional when it comes to important things. We're intentional about our finances, our relationships, the words we speak (hopefully—if not, read Matthew 12:36), and the time we give to our friendships and families and marriages. We're intentional about the things we value most in our lives, but very few of us are intentional about the mission of Christ. Strange, huh?

In the Gospels, we always see Jesus act with missional intentionality. In Mark 5, He was intentional in helping the Gerasene demoniac.

Jesus knew the demoniac was there, and He knew no one else had been able to help him. Scripture says that the community could not "subdue" him, the word in the Greek referring to one's efforts to suppress a wild beast. Their last resort, physically chaining him, was an utter disaster. Everything and everyone failed this man, and he was left alone among the dead to battle the demons.

Jesus knew the man's desperation.

The demoniac lived just across the lake from Jesus and the disciples, but this experience was way outside the disciples' social comfort zone. For an observant Jew, everything about this situation was unclean. The man was demon possessed and lived in the tombs, making him completely impure.[2] The swineherds in the area were another major defilement for Jews.[3] The pigs were being raised for the Roman occupiers of the region, making their presence a double offense, and the region was encompassed by Decapolis (the "ten cities"), a showcase for Hellenistic culture and ideas.

For the disciples, this area was as pagan as it got.

It's hard for us today to comprehend the profound nature of this situation. But if we're honest, we all understand the meaning of the word *unclean*. The unclean are people, neighborhoods, habits, scenarios, or lifestyles that we avoid. Unclean people may not live in our neighborhoods, but they aren't too far away.

Today their problems may be different, but they are desperate nonetheless—and no one knows what to do with them. Their friends, families, religions, churches, and communities have failed them. Socially and physically they have been cast to the side. Only Jesus can help these people.

The good news is that Jesus came to seek and save the lost. He put Himself in need of the woman at the well, touched the man with leprosy, and invited Himself to the home of a tax collector. Jesus intentionally looks for desperate people and intentionally works through His followers to reach them.

ALL THINGS NEW

In every gospel story we've looked at in this book, we've seen Jesus renewing lives. This is because the grand story of the Bible is essentially God making all things new. God will set right everything that's gone wrong. This is both a future reality and a present part of God's process.

Since Jesus' first coming, He has labored in the work of renewal. You and I are evidence of this process. "If anyone is in Christ, he is a new creature," says 2 Corinthians 5:17. "The old things passed away; behold, new things have come."

Jesus crossed a lake to renew the demoniac, but He made the greatest crossing—the divide between heaven and earth—to renew you and me. "The Word became flesh and blood, and moved into the neighborhood," says *The Message* paraphrase of John 1:14.

Christ initiated renewal for all people when He became flesh and completed the work at the cross where He died.

Every act of renewal Jesus initiates is led and accomplished by His Spirit. In fact, Jesus instructed His new creations to not even attempt to engage in mission until the Holy Spirit had come upon them.[4]

Jesus made it clear that there is no participation in His mission without the leading of the person of the Holy Spirit. The book of Acts exemplifies His Spirit's leading in the first thirty years of the church and gives a model to His church today.

In Acts 2, Peter was *filled with* the Holy Spirit, after which he preached the sermon at Pentecost that saw three thousand people saved.[5] In chapter 10, faith came to an entirely new community because Peter *heard* the Spirit say that three men were outside his house waiting to bring him to people who needed the gospel.[6] In chapter 13, Paul and Barnabas went on mission because the Holy Spirit *called* them during a worship service.[7] In chapter 16, Paul went to testify about Jesus with only the Spirit's *leading*.[8] Again and again we see Holy Spirit–led intentionality saturating the life of the early church.

The testimony of the church in Acts is that they were *filled with* the Spirit, they *heard* from the Spirit, the Spirit *called* them, and the Spirit *led* them on mission. The early Christians participated in Jesus' renewal of the world intentionally, and they were Spirit led in doing so.

FRUITFULNESS AND FRUSTRATION

Because we are modern witnesses to Jesus and the current manifestation of the church, the Bible says we should follow the Spirit's lead,[9] walk in the Spirit,[10] and continually be filled with the Spirit.[11] As we endeavor to live life at Godspeed, it's imperative that we learn how to hear what the Spirit says.[12]

The difference between hearing the Spirit and not hearing the Spirit on mission is the difference between fruitfulness and frustration.

Sometimes a person's need is immediately before us, and it's evident that we've been equipped to meet that need. In those times the mission is clear. But other times our brains will be of no help to us whatsoever. We will face situations such as driving past a teenage kid sitting on the side of a bridge, and we must obey the leading of the Holy Spirit and turn around.

In some ways that teenager on the curb was like the Gerasene demoniac. No one else could help him, and he was desperate. Seventy-eight cars drove past … before one family heard the voice of the Spirit and obeyed.

Jesus knew that teen was on the bridge, and He loves him and cares about his plight. Throughout history, for holy and inexplicable reasons, God has chosen to work *through* people in these situations rather than *independent of* people.

The mission of Christ is Christ's mission, not ours. And because it's His mission, He knows what He wants us to do.

So when it comes to Missio Christi, we don't get to make it up. It's not our mission. The task before us is to learn how to hear what the Holy Spirit says in order to discover what Jesus is already doing, and then we are to join Him.

If you've read this far into the book and are thinking, *Gosh, I've got to get out there and make this happen*, you're headed for fruitlessness and guilt.

Manufacturing mission will always lead to frustration.

But living at Godspeed is a God thing.

When we try to take mission into our own hands and "make it happen," we get discouraged. The mission doesn't work out for God's glory. We fail and feel guilty because we worked from a place of self-imposed religion instead of Holy Spirit leading.

The family who stopped to help the teen had learned how to hear the Holy Spirit when He spoke. But imagine if their methodology was to stop every time they saw a kid sitting on a curb. Would that have been more fruitful or more frustrating? More than likely they'd regularly be met with "Get out of my face!"

Do we believe in a God who is strategic, as history shows us He is? Do we believe in a God who is present, as the Bible tells us He is? Do we want to work with Him, or do we prefer our own hodgepodge of religious methodologies?

God created us for a purpose. He intended for our lives to count for something greater than ourselves, and His Spirit leads us for purposes both practical and eternal.

If you've been made new, Christ lives in you.[13] He wants to live His mission through you as the explanation and expression of who He is. Hearing from His Spirit is imperative to this participation process.

TEN EASY STEPS

Here's where most of us would like the "Ten Easy Steps to Being Led by the Holy Spirit." As Christians, we're anxious for a simple recipe.

If I wrote that book, it would probably sell a lot of copies. But I will never write that book. Here's why.

Learning to hear and follow the Spirit of God is part of the adventure and the mystery of the Christian life. The process of God is more relational, organic, and mystical than a manufactured list of ten easy steps. We crave automatic, but God created us for adventure.

Hearing from the Spirit is a lifelong process of discovery. The Bible reveals a God who is present, a God who speaks, a God who is intimately concerned with our lives, and a God who is willing to speak into our lives.

The good news is that there *are* specific things we can do to learn how to hear His Spirit's leading.

Beyond all doubt, Bible reading is indispensable to this Holy Spirit process. The Bible is the Word of God, and what God says to us will always line up with His Word. We begin to know the voice of God when we read and learn the Bible.

Communing with God in prayer is equally important. Prayer is more than just speaking to God—it's a conversation. Prayer involves listening, and how can you learn to know someone's voice unless you are within earshot? When we pray, we get within earshot of God.

Spirit-led mission is never *read these verses, pray this prayer, and voilà*.

While that would be easy, that's not how God works. To hear God speak, we must cultivate a relationship with the person of the Holy Spirit.

Prayer and Scripture are critical components to this relational process, and after that, it's trial and error. Sorry. The error part means we're going to make mistakes, and we need to be okay with that. We need to have grace for ourselves and for those around us when we mishear or don't hear at all from the Holy Spirit, because this is part of a lifelong and mysterious relationship with God. No one I know is batting a thousand when it comes to hearing the Spirit.

"To err is human," said Alexander Pope, and he's right.[14] God and His Word are infallible, but you and I are not.

You may think you hear the Spirit's leading (maybe it's audible or maybe it's a sense) and do something because of it. Maybe you go talk to the kid on the curb and he tells you to mind your own business, and you walk away thinking, *Oops. That wasn't it.* I can't tell you how many times this has happened in my life. This is why I was afraid during the launch of our new campus, Reality Santa Barbara, which I shared about in chapter 1. In the past I have heard the Spirit wrong or sometimes not at all.

But the next time comes, and you hear the Spirit of God, and you obediently do what He's leading you to do. This time you see fruit, beauty, renewal, mission, and Christ glorified. *That was it!*, you think. *That was His voice.* In this way you begin to learn, through trial and error, how to hear from the Holy Spirit.

In my experience, it helps me to hear from the Spirit when I get myself in a posture of praise and submission. When I'm desperate to hear God, I kneel or get flat on my face. When I force my physical self into a posture of worship, my spiritual self often follows. And when I rejoice in the cross, I am better prepared to hear and receive what the Spirit wants to say.

If you are already intentional about living your life on mission, this resonates. You know that you need the power and leading of the Spirit, and you understand this process of discovery. As mysterious as it may be, you know it is both real and possible, and you pursue it daily.

For those of you not living life on mission yet, this might feel alien to you. If you're concerned about your own plan, and if your mission is to please yourself, then you're probably hoping to preorder the *Ten Easy Steps* book. You desperately need to begin to cultivate a relationship with the person of the Holy Spirit. This starts with a humble submission of your will and your agenda to Him.

Jesus led His disciples to a place that wasn't far away—just across the water—but it was way outside their comfort zone. He led them there to renew a very tormented man.

Who around us is tormented today? Who is desperate? They might not live in our neighborhoods, but they're not too far away. They might seem a little foreign, even a little unclean. Maybe they're sitting on the side of a bridge.

How is the Spirit leading?

GO AND TELL

The Gerasene demoniac was a picture of the person whom Jesus intentionally went to on mission. More profoundly now, I want us to see the Gerasene man as a picture of us.

This man's story reveals what is true about all of us by nature apart from Jesus. We're slaves to evil, ultimately bent on self-destruction, and none of us are free apart from Christ. Jesus alone can break the power of sin and evil in our lives.

In the same way Jesus crossed the Sea of Galilee to heal this man, He crossed the divide between heaven and earth and came in the flesh to renew us through His cross and resurrection.

So what comes next? What happens between renewal and glory, between the time when we are born again and the day when we see Jesus face-to-face?

Put simply, God sends us into the world to testify about Jesus, just as He sent the demoniac back to his people to report the great things God had done.

Christianity is a "go and tell" life more than it is a "come and see" religion. Often Christians get together and say, "You want to check it out? Come see us." But our faith is based on the nature of God, who always reaches out in love. The pattern in Scripture is that God's activity is not one of entrenchment but of advancement.

When it comes to going and telling, there is no better person on earth to go and tell your friends, family, and coworkers about Jesus than you. You are the best person to report to your community about the great things the Lord has done and is doing in your life.

When you're living at Godspeed, going and telling look different in different situations. Sometimes you will proclaim and explain the gospel. Other times you will confront error and defend truth. Sometimes you'll do good and say nothing. Other times you'll do good and tell your story. Just like the former demoniac.

GOD IS NOT JEWISH

The first thing the early church did was report the work of Jesus. The Holy Spirit came upon them, and miraculously they began to speak in every tongue, and people from distant lands and languages heard about the wonderful works God had done.

Peter then turned to his own people, the Jews, and proclaimed the truth about Jesus. This is significant to the way God works. Just as it was with the former demoniac, sharing the gospel always starts with one's own people.

The first place Jesus went was to the lost house of Israel. Jesus instructed the disciples, who were Jewish, to start their mission in Jerusalem among their own people as well. Then they spread out to Samaria among those who were a little bit different than they were. And from there they went to the uttermost parts of the world, to people of every tribe and tongue across the globe.[15]

The disciples were the best people to reach their own people.

So it is with you and me.

We are part of our communities, so we don't have to do much homework to understand the society around us. We're immersed in it. We see the cultural analogies and the specific idols. We see any proclivities toward accepting God's truth and the things that are in direct opposition to it.

Your community is your people, and because they are your people, you understand their questions. What are they asking about God, eternity, and humanity? You understand their problems. What issues and challenges do they face? You understand their pain. Now how can you walk through their struggles with them?

They are your people, and because of that, you love them.

This concept is so obvious in the Bible that we often miss the profundity of it. Jesus wanted to reach Israel, so He came as a Jew. He identified with their culture, their religion, their issues, and their ideologies.

But God is not Jewish.

Jesus intentionally came to earth as a Jew. He strategically came to reach the Jewish people so that through them He might reach the entire world.

God is strategic. And we need to begin to see ourselves as strategically sent by God to our present time, place, context, and people. We are God's mission strategy.

We need to rid ourselves of the future-focused cultural mind-set that says "I will do it when ..." We claim we will make our lives about God's business when we attain our present goals, finish our schooling, and reach the right place in our career. We promise to serve the Lord when we have the right spouse, buy the right house, or own a new SUV.

God calls us on mission today.

But, you may be thinking, *the path that I took here was so messy and full of mistakes. This can't be where God has me on mission.*

Good news!

God is bigger than your mess and your mistakes.

No matter how muddled your life has been, God has a strategy to use you—as you are and where you are. He is bigger than your sin and is the One who redeems you. Your life is not the sum of your mistakes. God can use your mistakes. He is sovereign, and He sent you to this time and place strategically because you are the best person to reach the people around you.

LEAST LIKELY TO SUCCEED

The Gerasene demoniac was the very first person in Scripture to be sent out on mission by Jesus. That's a pretty unlikely first missionary! He's not who I would have chosen to send.

The guy had been demon possessed. He was crazy, to say the least—living among the graves, scraping his body with rocks, breaking his chains, naked, and screaming out constantly. He wasn't even a Jew! Yet this man, the *least* likely candidate, was the first person Jesus sent out on mission.

Those of us who are religious think, *Shouldn't you get this guy trained first? A few theology classes, some Bible 101, maybe a couple of solid years in a school of ministry?*

Yes, that would make sense. But that's not what Jesus did.

The man was healed, renewed, and sent; all these actions accomplished by Christ. What Jesus asked him to do wasn't complicated. Jesus said, "Go home and report to your people the great things the Lord has done for you." It doesn't require any training, because transformation is a witness that can be neither ignored nor denied.

If you've come to know Jesus, then there's real and evident change in your life. You are a different person today than before you met the Lord. Revealing this transformation is the goal of the Christian on mission. We are each a work in progress, but the process of transformation testifies to a work only Jesus can do. We need to communicate and display this process, this testimony, to our communities because the gospel is best heard where it is most clearly seen.

PERFECT FAKERS

Here's the problem: instead of communicating Holy Spirit transformation, the American church most often communicates a religion of rules and regulations.[16] This sets us up for failure in evangelization, because when it comes to keeping the rules, we're just not very good at it. I'm not anyway. Are you?

A recent study shows that born-again Christians are just as likely as non-Christians to view pornography, steal from others, physically fight and/or abuse someone, tell a lie, seek revenge, talk trash, get drunk, use drugs, and consult a medium or a psychic. These are statistical facts! We are, however, slightly less likely to cuss in public or to buy lottery tickets.[17]

Our lack of true sanctification, first and foremost, is a misrepresentation of the person of Christ. We wrongly tell the world that Christianity is a religion of rules—which it is not. Then, ironically, the world sees our actions and declares us hypocrites based on the standards we ourselves have put forward.

When we communicate that Christianity is about our performance—as opposed to Christ's work on the cross for us and the Spirit's transformation of us—we create the temptation in our churches and in our communities to fake it. We act like we have it all together and tell the world our faith is about keeping the rules.[18] Meanwhile, we break the rules ourselves and hide behind a facade.

The Bible says we don't have it all together, but Jesus does. We've performed horribly, but He's performed perfectly in our stead.

When we get saved, we don't become perfect people—we become *new* people.

CHOCOLATE-FACED

Jesus didn't give the former demoniac a list of rules to keep and standards to communicate. He just told him to share the story of what

God did for him. For those of us who are performance oriented, this is way too messy, risky, and unpolished.

Here is where you and I need to better understand our context. Analysis shows that young Americans distrust anything that seems too perfect. They expect life to be messy, flawed, and at times nonsensical.[19]

If as Christians we try to evangelize our communities by presenting a facade of perfection, we will totally miss the mark. We've failed to understand the gospel, and we've failed to understand our cultural context.

A commonly held perception about Christians today is that we analyze everyone else according to how they keep the rules and that we look down on others who perform poorly.

We're deeply flawed individuals who are seen as perfect only by God because we are in Christ. If the church is to participate effectively in the mission of Christ, it desperately needs to get humble, authentic, and transparent.

Transparency is the antidote to hypocrisy. As people, we have glaring inconsistencies and imperfections, and by trying to hide them, we look like little children with chocolate on our faces, claiming we didn't eat the cookie. Parents aren't fooled when their children tell a silly lie. Neither is the world fooled when the church pretends to be perfect.

Recently Toyota recalled over eight million vehicles for a gas-pedal malfunction, costing the company over two billion dollars. There was no hiding the blunder, so what did Toyota do? They launched a major marketing campaign in order to be transparent about the failure.[20]

I'm not touting this as authentic humility—it's smart marketing. But here's the point: marketing is aimed at addressing what people want most. A company like Toyota spent millions of dollars figuring out that what people want is transparency, humility, and authenticity. The corporate boardroom figured out what the American church is missing.

The Bible says we are a process. We *ought* to be more sanctified than we are—*absolutely*—but that's another book. When it comes to carrying out effective mission, it behooves us to simply be real and authentic with people. If we're going to talk about the mercy and forgiveness we receive, then we must be honest about why we need it.

WRIGLEY FIELD

Authentic transformation was Jesus' idea for communicating the gospel. That's why it works.

At the end of the story of the demoniac, the locals pleaded with Jesus to leave their region as He sent the formerly demon-possessed man on mission. In Mark 6, Jesus returned to the area, and this time everything had changed.

"Jesus!" the people exclaimed, "We know about You." In Mark 6 and 7, they brought every sick person they could find before Him to receive healing.[21] It was a paradigm shift, a community transformation. The people's perception of Jesus went from "Go away, we don't want You" to "We know You! We need You!"

All of this because one man went home to his people and reported the great things God had done in his life. The transformation of the Gerasene demoniac was real and authentic, and I imagine it was a witness of joy.

This man was possessed by a legion of demons—a legion is 6,826 soldiers in Roman military count—and now he had been made new. He must have radiated joy.[22] He wasn't going to his people a perfect man; he was going to them a *new* man. That's worth getting excited about.

Recently I met up with a group of pastors in Chicago and was invited to join them for a Chicago Cubs game. Now I'd never been to a baseball game in my entire life (no, honestly—and I'm sorry if that lowers your opinion of me), and I can't say I'm inspired to go to many more (sorry, America).

We went to a place called Wrigley Field, which I'm told is a big deal. The place just seemed a bit old and outdated to me. We sat in something called a box above first base, which was supposed to be exciting. But, through the course of the entire game, almost no one ever got to first base. I mean, just first base! For hours I was bored out of my mind.

At last the game ended.

As we walked to the parking lot, people everywhere chanted a song about the Cubs and their great victory. Thousands of them, in unison, just sang and sang and sang. It was crazy! One of the pastors turned to me and said, "These people are more excited about the Cubs than Christians are about the resurrection of Jesus Christ."

He was right!

Not even the people at Hillsong United worship events compete with Chicago Cubs fans after a victory. These people were insane for their cause. Afterward you could hear them in the streets, honking and cheering, "They won! Hooray!" The report went out throughout all of Chicago. Victory was in the air.

Church, where is our joy? Where is our excitement? What is our witness to the victory of Christ?

YOU ARE AN EVANGELIST

Everyone is an evangelist for something.

You evangelize for whatever you're most excited about. If I go to your Facebook page, if I read your Twitter posts, if I check out your blog, I'm going to figure out what you get most excited about. If I spend just a few moments on your social-network pages, your greatest passions will likely be obvious.

If we've truly experienced the transformation of Christ, then we have the greatest opportunity to communicate to our communities about who Jesus is. And our communities are the context to which we've been sent by God.

If we've experienced renewal by the power of the Holy Spirit, then let's live out our mission with transparency, authenticity, and irrepressible joy.

The world—especially your friends—is waiting for your witness.

10

KINGDOM

The Upside-Down Order

We talk about heaven being so far away. It is within speaking distance to those who belong there.

Dwight L. Moody

One of the many stories posted on MissioChristi.net came from a practicing lawyer in our congregation. She worked at a firm where the people coming to her needed more than just legal wins.

She saw that they were broken people in desperate need.

For two years she prayed for God's direction and felt the Lord leading her to leave her comfortable position and paycheck for something bigger. God called her on mission to start her own firm, where she could care for people with a kingdom mind-set.

And wouldn't you know it? The moment she quit her job at the lucrative firm, her husband lost his job. It takes such faith to be on mission sometimes.

Without financial backing or a safety net, this woman launched a new law firm. She wrote on the Missio Christi website, "I have a duty not to 'prey on the flock' but to protect, defend and nourish the people God sends me.… I know I have a grave responsibility now."

The first person she hired at the firm was a full-time intercessor: a woman she paid to pray for the clients, cases, and courts. Yes, you read that correctly.

"We have had amazing results," she continued. "I have had some fantastic legal wins and I can say they are the result of prayer.... This ministry awes me. I am so freed! ... I understand that the people who come here are broken; I am able to witness to them in deed and in word."[1]

The kingdom of God reverses the world's order of priorities. One lawyer reverted from making decisions according to how lucrative they might be and reformed her business to be about helping people. She still makes money, but now she is caring for people in a radical kingdom way.

When we follow Jesus on mission, servanthood and sacrifice come first, because the kingdom of God is an upside-down kingdom.

JESUS AND THE KINGDOM

John the Baptist baptized Jesus in the River Jordan. When He came out of the water, Jesus saw heaven torn open and the Holy Spirit descending upon Him like a dove.

"You are My beloved Son," came a voice from heaven. "In You I am well-pleased."

At once the Holy Spirit sent Jesus into the wilderness. Satan tested Jesus for forty days, and angels attended Him. During that time, the government took John the Baptist into custody and put him in prison. When Jesus came out of the wilderness, He went down into Galilee, preaching the gospel.

The ministry of Christ had begun.

"The time is fulfilled," Jesus proclaimed to the people, "and the kingdom of God is at hand; repent and believe in the gospel."

Then Jesus called His first disciples.[2]

THREE TENSES

When Jesus came, He brought the kingdom.

"The time is fulfilled" were the first words proclaimed in His ministry. "The kingdom of God is at hand."

Many Christians imagine the kingdom of God as the celestial city we'll inhabit in heaven. But it's not. It's so much more.

The kingdom is the rule and the reign of God, in heaven *and* on earth. This is what Jesus ushered in at the outset of His ministry. The kingdom came in a peculiar way at the first coming of Christ, it is coming in fullness at the second coming of Christ, and it works presently in and through us by the power of Christ.

It helps me to understand the kingdom when I think about it in its three tenses: historical (past), practical (present), and eschatological (future).

The three tenses of the kingdom make sense when we consider the three tenses of Christian salvation: God saved us from the penalty of sin (past), we are being saved daily from the power of sin (present), and we will be forever saved from the presence of sin (future). Jesus won the victory at the cross, but the results of our believing the gospel unfold in three tenses throughout history and over the course of our lives.

Think about what happens when we go out on mission: our ministry follows the same three tenses! We preach the historical fact of Christ crucified and resurrected (past), we demonstrate and display the life of Christ through us (present), and we point the world to the consummation, completion, and renewal of all things (future).

There is a finish, and that finish is Christ Himself.

THE KING

The Bible mentions the kingdom of God and its synonym, the kingdom of heaven, over eighty times in the New Testament. It was the focus of Christ's ministry and message, and therefore it follows: the kingdom must be the framework for our lives on mission.

As the church, we cannot talk about mission without thinking about the kingdom of God. And we cannot think about the kingdom of God until we realize that it's all about the King.

"Blessed is the King who comes in the name of the Lord," the people of Jerusalem sang at Jesus' triumphal entry.[3] This moment was the fulfillment of the prophecy in Zechariah 9:9: "Behold, your King is coming to you … humble, and mounted on a donkey."

Jesus came as King, but He came in a peculiar way.[4] He came in an *unkingly* sort of fashion. The character of the King and the way in which He came are indicative of what the kingdom will look like. Jesus came as a baby and rode in on a donkey precisely because He was ushering in a kingdom of humility.

And Christ is coming again. But according to Scripture, when He returns this time, He won't be coming humbly.

Matthew 24:30 says that when Jesus returns, it will be with power and in great glory. On His robe and thigh will be written the name "King of Kings and Lord of Lords,"[5] and at that time "every tongue will confess that Jesus Christ is Lord, to the glory of God the Father."[6]

The kingdom, again, will look like the King.

Many Christians use *the kingdom of God* as a synonym for heaven or the hereafter. That's a misunderstanding. The kingdom of God exists in time and space *among humanity*; it is the rule and reign of Christ.

At Jesus' first coming, the kingdom was inaugurated, broke into history, and manifested in our context here on earth. When Jesus returns, the kingdom will break into history once more, this time in fullness.

For this reason, the kingdom of God is both here and still coming, both present and future, already and not yet.

WRONG ALLEGIANCES

God has always been King. The Old Testament calls Him the King of the universe—the *melekh ha'olam*, in Hebrew. The Israelites historically longed for their King to bring His authority, rule, and reign to earth. When Jesus came the first time, this is exactly what He did. He came as the King, inaugurating the kingdom, and said, "The time is fulfilled."

We may not have kings in America, but we understand that a king demands allegiance, and allegiance requires loyalty and commitment. When Christ comes, He calls humanity to allegiance by way of repentance. "The kingdom of God is at hand; repent and believe in the gospel."

When Jesus came as King, He brought light into the darkness of the world. Matthew quotes the Old Testament prophecy about His coming, saying, "The people who were sitting in darkness saw a great light, and those who were sitting in the land and shadow of death, upon them a light dawned."[7]

The reason why humanity suffers in darkness—in the shadow of death—is because of wrong allegiances. These allegiances are the very things from which Christ called humanity to repent.

You see, the Bible identifies Satan as the ruler of this world.[8] He is not the ruler by right (he is not the king), but he is the de facto ruler by way of allegiance because men and women have wittingly and unwittingly pledged their loyalty to him. Jesus said that Satan came to kill, steal, and destroy.[9] He keeps people enslaved to sin,[10] and his reign is a reign of death.[11]

Satan may be the de facto ruler of earth, but Jesus is the true and only King of the universe.

"The Son of God appeared for this purpose," says 1 John 3:8, "to destroy the works of the devil." Christ came to bring life where there was death,[12] light where there was darkness,[13] and freedom where there was bondage.[14] Jesus calls men and women to enter that kingdom through a change in allegiance—*through repentance.*

Repent is such a beautiful word.

Repentance was Jesus' first demand upon humanity—the first instruction of His public ministry.[15] To repent is to undergo a full change of mind and heart that causes a radical change in life direction and behavior. Repentance is the change of allegiance by which we come out of darkness into light, out of death into life.

Humanity must repent of wrong allegiances to dead works and wrong allegiances to dead idols.[16]

Dead works—such as immorality, impurity, enmities, and strife—are the sins of the flesh that keep us from relationship with God. These sins, listed in Galatians 5:19–21, and all sin, lead to death and separation from a holy God.

Dead idols are anyone or anything that shapes our thinking and behavior more than Christ. If I'm driven by the pursuit of money, or the well-being of my family, or my relationship with other people, and that pursuit takes Christ's place of preeminence in my life, then that person or thing has become my idol. Idols aren't always things that are intrinsically bad. Often they are good things that we have simply assigned too much importance to.

We must repent of our allegiances, because in the kingdom of God dual allegiances don't exist.[17] Our loyalty to dead works and dead idols has made us spiritually dead, but by the work of Jesus on the cross, we can be made spiritually alive again.[18]

This is the gospel.

"I tell you the truth," Jesus said, "unless you are born again, you cannot see the Kingdom of God."[19]

Repentance is radical. Colossians 1:13 says when we repent, we are rescued from the domain of darkness and brought into the kingdom of the beloved Son. When we change allegiance by repentance, we are rescued from the sins that brought us into death, and we come under the rule and the reign of the true King, Jesus Christ.

We gain entry into the kingdom by repentance, and then we participate in its spread across the world by living life at Godspeed.

WHEN GOD GETS HIS WAY

The incarnation of Jesus is the beginning of the revelation of God's character to humanity. "No one has seen God at any time ..." says John 1:18, "but [Christ] has explained Him."

In the same way, the kingdom functioning in our world should help explain to others who God is. When you and I do kingdom ministry and mission, that work is an illustration of what the world looks like when God gets His way.

Jesus also did away with the false dualism of the sacred and the secular. The incarnation shows that God cares about both, because God, who is Spirit, draped Himself in human flesh in order to reach humanity. The physical and the spiritual are intermingled, and in doing kingdom work, Jesus removes the separation. He approaches mission holistically.

The Greek word for *salvation* (*sozo*) means to "heal" or "make whole." This word is used throughout Jesus' ministry in the Gospels to describe both physical healings and the eternal forgiveness of sins.[20]

The New Testament writers made the same holistic application to Old Testament prophecy. Matthew, in chapter 8 of his gospel, applied the prophecy of Isaiah 53:5 to *physical* healing: "They brought to Him many who were demon-possessed; and He cast out the spirits with a word, and healed all who were ill. This was to fulfill what was spoken through Isaiah the prophet: 'He Himself took our infirmities and carried away our diseases.'"[21] Then Peter, in chapter 2 of his first epistle, applied the same Isaiah 53:5 prophecy to *spiritual* healing in speaking about redemption.[22] When Jesus heals, it is biblically understood as both physical and spiritual.

This holistic approach to ministry extends to Christ's mission today. The church is called to minister to impoverished people, meaning those in physical poverty—without resources, opportunities, connectivity, or possibilities—as well as the spiritually impoverished all around us. When the New Testament speaks of injustice and captivity, it explains how God deals with both the spiritual and the physical manifestations.[23] In Jesus' ministry, He addressed both physical blindness[24] and spiritual blindness.[25] He came to the nationally oppressed (Israel) and the spiritually oppressed (the demonized).

When God gets His way, it always has both physical implications and spiritual implications. The church is on mission to both matters of the physical and the spiritual because both needs surround us. And as members of the kingdom, we get to meet the needs of humanity in the same way that Jesus did: *by the power of the Holy Spirit.*

WOODEN SPOON REMINDER

Jesus proclaimed the good news everywhere He went. "Let us go somewhere else to the towns nearby, so that I may preach there also," He said to His disciples. "For that is what I came for."[26]

My daughter, Daisy Love, understands the importance of preaching the gospel in Christian mission.

The week I shared this message at Reality, I came home from work one evening with lackluster energy. It had been a long day, and after giving Daisy a hug in the living room, I sauntered over to the kitchen counter where Kate had prepared our meal.

"Sweetie, how was your day?" she asked.

I plopped my things down and began recounting the day's events. "Oh, I had this meeting and it went forever … and then I had that meeting I told you about … and then I met with so-and-so … and then I had another meeting … and then I met with this guy."

As I talked, five-year-old Daisy got up from her seat in the living room, went into the kitchen, and pulled out a wooden spoon. (She remembers where they are, because she sees Daddy get them out frequently for use on her big brother.) I didn't pay much attention to what she was doing, continuing on about the meetings, until all of a sudden—

Smack!

Daisy had whacked me with a wooden spoon, right on the rear end.

"Oh!" I turned around in surprise, "Daisy, what are you doing? Why are you spanking Daddy?"

My five-year-old daughter looked straight up at me, shaking the spoon. "'Cause you didn't preach the gospel today, Daddy," she said. "You only had meetings. You're supposed to preach the gospel!"

Who is this kid? I thought as she gave me another smack on the rear.

"Okay, sweetie, I'll preach the gospel."

Little Daisy Love gets the importance of something that the church needs to be more passionate about: *the proclamation of the kingdom of God and the preaching of the gospel.*

And Jesus did more than just preach the gospel—He put it on display! Through signs, wonders, healings, compassion, mercy, and resurrections. Our mission follows the mission of Jesus, and Jesus gave attention to *both* proclamation *and* demonstration in bringing forth the kingdom.

The modern church divides itself over demonstration and proclamation, liberal and conservative—and in the arguing, both sides miss something of the person of Christ.

The demonstration illustrates the proclamation, and the proclamation explains the demonstration.

STUFF OF THE KINGDOM

When the King gets His way, poverty, sickness, injustice, and oppression go away—by the power of Holy Spirit, through the proclamation and demonstration of the gospel. As members of God's kingdom, we participate in this work.

Not long ago Iranian officials arrested two women in Iran merely for being Christian. They went before a judge, who told them they'd be set free if they simply denounced their faith.

"We believe in Jesus," they said, and the judge put them in prison as a result.

Then came the International Day of Prayer for the Persecuted Church. Reality, along with countless other churches across the globe, prayed specifically for these women. That very week in Iran, after 259 days in prison, these two sisters in Christ were set free.[27]

This miracle is the stuff of the kingdom. We partner with God in His work against physical manifestations of oppression and injustice, and we do this with spiritual manifestations of oppression and injustice as well.

One of Reality's church plants is in Stockton, California, which *Forbes* recently named the number one most miserable city to live in America.[28] (Hooray!) Reality Stockton launched well, and they had just opened their second campus when I was awoken one night by a text message from the pastor.

"We just cast a bunch of demons out of a girl at our prayer meeting. She's been set free."

"Are you okay?" I responded.

"Yeah, I'm on fire," the pastor wrote. "I'm so stoked. This is the third person at the new campus that we've had to cast demons out of."

This is the stuff of the kingdom. Whether the oppression and injustice manifest themselves in physical ways (like our sisters in

Iran) or spiritual ways (like the demonic opposition in Stockton), the church deals with both by the power of the Holy Spirit.

We, as people of the kingdom, are a present explanation of what it looks like when the King gets His way. We participate, and this work gives a foretaste of the freedom that will exist in fullness when Jesus comes again.

OPPOSITES DAY

Every so often when our family sits down to dinner, my son, Isaiah, will look at his plate full of broccoli (which he hates) and say with the biggest grin, "Oh, I love broccoli! And I hate surfing."

Immediately we know that it's Opposites Day. The entire family will join with my son in saying and doing all kinds of things that are opposite. It's so fun.

Soon there will be an Opposites Day in the kingdom of God. A day of reversal, when those who were first will be last and those who were last will be first.[29]

The priorities of our society are power and influence, but the priorities of the kingdom are servanthood and sacrifice.[30] These opposites are indicative of the great reversal that is coming.

As we go forward on mission, we manifest this opposite reality in the world—the reversal of values that exists in the upside-down kingdom. One family shared this story of reversal on the Missio Christi website:

> We had a fun but different Thanksgiving. Being fairly new to Santa Barbara, we wanted to have a great first Thanksgiving here. We invited our

family/friends from CO and TX and did not have anyone that accepted our invitation. So we took it to the streets … we went down to the wharf on Thanksgiving morning and asked several homeless men if they had planned on attending the Veteran's meal. They said, "No, [we don't] want to go.…" So we asked them if they would like to have a meal with us at the end of the wharf on the picnic tables. Their eyes lit up and they said, "Yes, that would be great … what time?"

I said maybe around 12:30? So we went to the store, got the turkey, etc., etc., and prepared all the sides … took it to the tables at about 12:15 … set out a table cloth and decked it with the full banquet and Thanksgiving Day greeting cards from the kids.

At 12:25 I set out to gather up some of the guys … little did I know that they were already on their way to our table. When I got to the end of the wharf, I started asking [more] homeless people to come and they all responded by saying, "Yeah, we know about it, and we are headed up there in a bit." At this point, I knew something was up and I rushed back only to find a line of guys waiting at our table with open hands and smiles on their faces. They had arrived at precisely 12:30!

We fed many people … and we prayed and shared Jesus with a lot of new friends.[31]

This is the stuff of the kingdom. It's tangible, immediate, doable, profound, and it's just what Jesus said the kingdom would be like.

In Luke 14, Jesus used a parable to explain the kingdom of God. He told the story of a man who invites all the rich and important people he knows to his banquet.

But none of them come.

So the man tells his servants, "Go out at once into the streets and lanes of the city and bring in here the poor and crippled and blind and lame." These are the types of people, Jesus illustrated, who will be found at His banquet table in the kingdom.[32]

In the same way, the family in our church did the work of the kingdom when they brought their Thanksgiving table to people in their community who were in need.

The apostle Paul, when explaining his approach to mission in 1 Corinthians 10, wrote, "[I'm] not seeking my own profit but the profit of the many, so that they may be saved."[33] I love that picture. The kingdom mind-set actively seeks the profit of others, for the good of all people and the furtherance of the kingdom.

Romans 14:17 says, "The kingdom of God is … righteousness and peace and joy in the Holy Spirit." So how do we, by the power of the Holy Spirit, bring righteousness where it isn't? How do we bring peace where there's turmoil? How do we bring joy where there's sorrow?

BETWEEN TWO ARRIVALS

In the kingdom we have victory. Jesus set us free from the bondage, burden, and allegiance to sin. "Everyone who commits sin is a slave of sin," said Jesus, "[but] if the Son makes you free, you will be free indeed."[34]

We also have victory over demonic opposition and over Satan and his schemes. Jesus announced, "If I cast out demons by the Spirit of God, then the kingdom of God has come upon you."[35]

The kingdom comes with the authority of the King, Jesus Christ, who is far and above any other ruler, power, or principality. Jesus gives His followers this same authority. In Luke 10, He sent out His disciples on a practice mission trip, and they came back rejoicing: "Lord, even the demons are subject to us in Your name."[36]

In preparing His disciples for the trip, Jesus had instructed them, "Whatever city you enter and they receive you, eat what is set before you; and heal those in it who are sick, and say to them, 'The kingdom of God has come near to you.'"[37]

We have victory over sin. We have victory over Satan. And we have victory over sickness. These victories are attributes of the kingdom, and these victories should be real, concrete experiences in our lives.

But … we also live between the two comings of Christ. The King came in a peculiar way before, and the King will come in a particular way in the future. We experience some of the kingdom right now, but we won't experience the fullness of the kingdom until He comes again.

Jesus dealt with sin, death, and the devil when He came to earth; and He defeated them all at the cross and in His resurrection. Yet we still experience those things, don't we? Been tempted lately? I thought so. Me too. We see traces of complete victory and restoration in these areas, but we do not always see the fullness of the victory. Similarly we aren't always healed, are we? Believe me, as the father of a child battling cancer, I wish God always provided immediate physical healing. But He doesn't. Not always. Sometimes we suffer, and that's okay. The kingdom is here and Christ is present in us so that we do not suffer alone. But the King is coming to right every wrong and make all things new, and soon we will not suffer at all.

What we experience currently in the kingdom is good news: the power of Christ working in and through His people. What we'll experience in the coming kingdom is even better news. At the second coming, the world will become the domain of Christ. As Revelation 11:15 reveals, "The kingdom of the world [will] become the kingdom of our Lord."

The devil was defeated at the cross but will be tormented at Christ's second coming. Jesus broke sin's power and defeated death at the cross and resurrection, but when Jesus comes again, these things will be abolished forever. Healing has been provided but will be perfected at His next arrival.

A tangible tension resides between these two comings of Christ, and this puts us today in the age of hope.

"Three things will last forever," says 1 Corinthians, "faith, hope, and love."[38]

Humanity survives on hope, and hope is the very expectation that something good will come.

VICTORY AND SUFFERING

Wherever hope exists, suffering exists also; for if there's no suffering, then there's no need for hope.

Suffering is a component of the current kingdom. In fact, we're able to enter into the kingdom only because of the King's suffering on the cross. Jesus didn't do away with the suffering of the world at

His first coming. That is yet to come. What He did away with was the separation between the world and a holy God.

When we enter into the kingdom of God, we become a part of the fellowship of Christ's sufferings.[39] We have hope because we look forward to the day when Jesus will wipe away every tear and eradicate all death, mourning, crying, and pain.[40]

Jesus will deal with the suffering of humanity, and so we say the words of 2 Corinthians 4:16–17: "We do not lose heart, but though our outer man is decaying, yet our inner man is being renewed day by day. For our momentary, light affliction is producing for us an eternal weight of glory far beyond all comparison."

As Christians on mission, we don't view suffering as the world views suffering. The kingdom of God gives us a present and future theology of victory over sin, Satan, and sickness based upon the death and resurrection of Christ. "I consider that the sufferings of this present time are not worthy to be compared with the glory that is to be revealed to us," Paul wrote in Romans 8:18.

The kingdom gives us both a theology of victory and a theology of suffering, the two expressed equally throughout the New Testament.

In Matthew 16, Peter struggled with the fact that Christ was going to be crucified and that the kingdom of God would involve suffering. "If anyone wishes to come after Me," Jesus said to His disciples, "he must deny himself, and take up his cross and follow Me."[41] In that culture the phrase *take up your cross* meant nothing less than suffering and death.

"For whoever wishes to save his life will lose it," Jesus continued. "But whoever loses his life for My sake will find it."[42]

For the apostle Paul, being on mission meant that he faced some real hardship and suffering:

> Five times I received from the Jews thirty-nine lashes. Three times I was beaten with rods, once I was stoned, three times I was shipwrecked, a night and a day I have spent in the deep. I have been on frequent journeys, in dangers from rivers, dangers from robbers, dangers from my countrymen, dangers from the Gentiles, dangers in the city, dangers in the wilderness, dangers on the sea, dangers among false brethren; I have been in labor and hardship, through many sleepless nights, in hunger and thirst, often without food, in cold and exposure. Apart from such external things, there is the daily pressure on me of concern for all the churches.[43]

Addressing the church in Acts 14, Paul wrote, "Through many tribulations we must enter the kingdom of God."[44] He knew this truth through suffering; because in the midst of suffering, we experience the power of the kingdom.

We enter in.

The never-ending reverberation of the New Testament is to endure hardship.[45] Christ even said that those who endure and overcome will reign with Him.[46] If you haven't heard the repeated encouragement for the church to endure in the midst of suffering, then I encourage you to read the New Testament again.

The call to endure prepares us to maintain allegiance to the King in every circumstance. For what is allegiance unless it's been tried? What is loyalty or commitment unless it's been tested?

THE PURPOSE AND PRIZE

The Bible holds these kingdom realities in tension: humility and power, suffering and victory.

This tension keeps us from false expectations and theological tweaking. We know that the kingdom comes with victory—power, signs, and wonders—but we're not obsessed with them. We know that in the kingdom we will experience suffering, but we also expect to experience Christ's healing, deliverance, and victory.

We live in this tension because the kingdom is both present and forthcoming.

In my daughter's struggle with cancer, she has suffered immensely, and so has our entire family.

Yet through her suffering, we've witnessed the kingdom of God go forth in ways we've never seen before. We've seen untold numbers of people who had outright rejected the gospel tell us they are now considering Christ because of the faith they've seen in our little girl. Some prodigals came to me and said, "I was far off from Jesus, and then I heard about Daisy. I was prompted to pray, and my life has been revived. I am on fire for Christ like I haven't been in years."

One evening Kate brought Daisy down to the beach while I was surfing. A woman came up to them as they walked; she was so excited to meet our daughter.

"You know, before I heard about what Daisy was going through and her suffering, I had no prayer life," the woman told my wife. "I just didn't know how to pray. But for some reason, I started praying for your little girl—and my world has changed. Now I pray for everything, all the time."

This is the theology of suffering. It's the stuff of the kingdom.

I have experienced the victory too. My mother had a lump in her breast, which the doctors were going to remove. We prayed for God to intervene, and she told the doctors, "Test one more time." They tested her once more before surgery, and the lump was gone.

This kind of victory is entirely of the kingdom—and it's the kingdom work we love to see. But I have experienced more of Christ in pain and suffering than I ever have in seasons of ease and comfort. I've discovered that Christ is most beautiful when we are most broken. Wonderfully, God is present in our pain.

The presence of others is sweeter in suffering too—because suffering binds people together. Think about soldiers who have fought and suffered together on the front lines of battle and the lifelong bonds they built as a result. If success bound people together, the Beatles never would have broken up.

Both the theology of victory and the theology of suffering bring glory to God, for Christ redeems them both. Yet when we understand the *upside-downness* of the kingdom, that the King Himself suffered and that we too will suffer, we are truly able to say, "Christ is glorified in my weakness."[47]

Church, the question before us is this: Will we remain allegiant to the King?

Will we be faithful, even when we're experiencing the reverberations of the domain of darkness and the effects of sin and evil in this world? Will we follow Jesus when He, in His infinite wisdom and love, allows a measure of suffering in our lives (as the Bible says He will)?

Knowing that the kingdom is here now keeps us from letting the difficulties of this life rule over us, because Christ rules over them all. And knowing that the kingdom is still coming keeps us from losing heart, because we know that eventually Christ will right every wrong and reverse every evil.

The ultimate purpose of the mission of Jesus and the coming of the kingdom of God is to bring us to the King Himself.

Christ is our prize.

The kingdom is not merely about the signs and wonders and the victory, nor is it about the pain and the suffering and the ministry. *Jesus is enough.*

In sickness and in health, in poverty and in wealth, Christ is the treasure of our lives.

The kingdom has come that we might come to the King.

11

PRAY

The Battle Lines and Bean Fields

We can reach our world, if we will.
The greatest lack today is not people or
funds. The greatest need is prayer.

Wesley L. Duewel

Not long ago a story flooded international news about two American journalists captured on the border of North Korea. North Koreans held the women captive and sentenced them to eleven years in a military labor camp.

One of the women was a member of our Reality church plant in Los Angeles, where she attended regularly with her husband and children.

Her situation was one of clear injustice and governmental oppression, and the church responded in the most powerful way that it could: it hit its knees.

Reality Los Angeles prayed incessantly for the release of these women. Day and night they cried out to the King that justice would be done and that these two would be restored to their families and community.

What happened?

Bill Clinton himself got on a plane, went to North Korea, and brought the women home. Praise God!

Our government took action, and I have no doubt there were significant political discussions to negotiate such a release. But the salient, missional point is that the church did something. The Christian brothers and sisters of these women confronted the injustice against them.

They participated in the going forth of the kingdom of God, through the most powerful weapon of the church.

JESUS AND PRAYER

Jesus went away to a certain place to pray to the Father.

When He returned to His disciples, they asked Him for the first time to teach them something specifically: "Lord," one of the disciples implored, "teach us to pray."[1]

ANYTHING

If you were face-to-face with Jesus and could ask Him to teach you *anything*, what would it be?

There are so many things I would want to learn.

As a surfer, I would say, "Jesus, teach me that walking on water thing." Being a mourner, I would say, "Jesus, teach me to raise people from the dead." Being a father whose daughter had cancer, I would say, "Jesus, teach me how to heal people miraculously."

The disciples had the opportunity to ask Jesus, the Son of God, to teach them *anything*. The single request they made was "Lord, teach us to pray."

When we read the Gospels, we see Jesus praying often and continuously. He would go away to pray in the morning.[2] He would go off by Himself to pray in the evening.[3] He would leave His followers and pray alone all night long.[4]

The disciples saw Jesus do innumerable miraculous things. Yet they witnessed prayer to be His key habit, forming the rhythm of His life. Prayer was the source from which everything else flowed. For the people who observed Jesus' life day in and day out, prayer appeared to be the most profound thing He did.

"Lord, teach us to pray."

This was the only time in all of the Gospels that the disciples directly asked Jesus to teach them anything. Prayer was the game changer, and the disciples saw that Jesus depended on it.

In modeling its mission after Jesus, the early church also defined itself by its propensity to pray. We are told in Acts 1:14 and again in Acts 2:42 that the followers in the church "were continually devoting themselves to prayer."

When we look at Jesus, and when we look at the early church, we see that the mission of Christ is soaked in prayer.

As you and I endeavor to live lives at Godspeed, like Jesus did, it is imperative that we learn to pray. And pray often.

PRAYER CHANGES THINGS

The prayer life of the church develops when we realize things *change* when we pray.

Every time the Bible mentions prayer, it talks about people, situations, circumstances, forces of wickedness and their influence, cities, and even nations *changing*.

God moves in response to our prayers. This is not a violation of His sovereignty but rather an expression of it. This is an illumination of just how relational God is. He *wants* to hear our voices. Our prayers are like golden bowls of incense, pleasing before Him.[5]

So when we pray, in some mysterious way, it moves the hand of God. And when we don't pray, the opposite occurs. "You do not have because you do not ask," Scripture says.[6]

In Exodus 32, God was going to judge the nation of Israel for their idolatry. In His holy justice He was going to destroy them, and they deserved it. But Moses stood in the gap. He prayed, "God, have mercy on them." And do you know what it says right there in Exodus 32?

"So the Lord changed His mind."[7]

One man pleaded the case of Israel before God, and it rerouted the course of history.

This is uncomfortable theological ground: God changing His mind? It's uncomfortable because we know when and under what conditions we change our own minds. Either we change our minds because we lack knowledge or information or we were incorrect in our assumptions and we made a mistake.

God never has a lack of knowledge—He knows all things, from beginning to end, actual and possible. God also never makes mistakes—He's perfect and holy all the time. So God doesn't change His mind like we change our minds.

When Scripture says God changed His mind, it means that He relented from an undesirable course of action. God planned to judge the people of Israel because He is just, and justice is what they deserved. Yet it was an undesirable course because He is also a merciful God, and He wants to extend His mercy. When one man pleaded on behalf of the people, God decided to spare Israel.

All it took was someone willing to ask.

Conversely look at Ezekiel 22. God was going to judge His people, because (once again) they deserved it. Being perfectly just, yet merciful, God looked for someone—*anyone!*—who would stand in the gap and intercede on behalf of the people.

This time He found no one.

So God judged the nation.[8]

God presently and historically commits Himself to our prayers in this powerful way—how radical! And yet, He never violates His own will, and this is the confidence we have before Him: if we ask anything according to the will of God, we will have the thing for which we have asked.[9]

With this powerful thing called prayer comes a tremendous responsibility. If prayer *truly* changes things—if it changes the plights of people and situations and whole nations, if it pushes back evil and brings the merciful hand of God—then we, as the Lord's ambassadors, have a moral obligation to pray.

BATTLE LINES

We have been given a mandate by Jesus to take the gospel into the world. "Go therefore and make disciples of all the nations," Jesus said in Matthew 28, "baptizing them in the name of the Father and the Son and the Holy Spirit, teaching them to observe all that I have commanded you."

This is the Great Commission.

"And lo, I am with you always," Jesus concluded, "even to the end of the age."[10]

Jesus directly connects His presence in our lives to our living on mission with Him. He commanded us to go make disciples, baptize, teach, and preach the gospel. And in that context, as we endeavor to stay on mission, He will be with us always.

The presence of Christ is the context for mission.

Living at Godspeed means we experience a profound, practical sense of Christ with us. This is different than our understanding of God as omnipresent or as showing up when "two or more are gathered." I'm talking about a tangible, manifest, discernible, and practical presence of Christ in our lives. Jesus promised this.

If you're already living on mission, you realize the challenges and obstacles before you. The enormity of the task at hand makes us *desperate* for the presence of Jesus. The more we live on mission, the more we realize our own frailty and weakness and the more we want (and need) Christ with us.

Hudson Taylor, that great missionary to China, once said, "All God's giants have been weak men who did great things for God because they reckoned on God being with them."[11]

The saints to whom Taylor referred were ordinary people who laid hold of the promise of the Great Commission: *if we live life on mission, Jesus will be with us.* They were weak men and women enabled to do great things for the glory of God.

Consider then what Charles Spurgeon said about the manifest, practical presence of God: "If God be near a church, it must pray. And if he be not there, one of the first tokens of his absence will be a slothfulness in prayer."[12]

When God is near people, those people want to talk to God. When that tangible, manifest presence of God is missing, the desire to pray is missing as well.

Apply this principle to the individual Christian: if God is present in the person's life in a profound way—practically and intimately—the result is going to be prayer.

Prayer is our gauge of God's presence.

If you feel a burden to pray and you find yourself speaking to God—*calling out to God*—then God is near to you. You are experiencing the person of Christ. If you aren't clinging to Jesus in a practical, tangible way, the first sign will be your lack of desire to talk to Him—what Spurgeon called "a slothfulness in prayer."

When we live at Godspeed, we experience the promise of Jesus' presence. This moves us to pray as we get deeper into mission. We have an intimate, profound, and powerful experience of the person of Christ in us, through us, and with us.

Those who are Christians in name only, who live for their own glory and their own purposes, may wonder at this concept. They often lack the missional presence of Christ because they haven't created a need for the promise of Matthew 28—"I am with you always"—to be fulfilled.

These nominal or "Sunday" Christians do not experience the power of God in their daily lives because they are *missing* mission. There is no need for the unique presence and aroma of Christ, because they're not taking Christ to people. They're not seeking to share Him, and thus, they lack any sense of living on the front lines—in their families, in their marriages, with their kids, in their communities, in their workplaces, in their schools—*anywhere*.

Jim Cymbala, in *Fresh Wind, Fresh Fire*, put it this way:

> When it comes to spiritual matters, you and I will never know our potential under God until we step out and take risks on the front line of battle. We will never see what power and anointing are possible until we bond with our King and go out in

> his name to establish his kingdom. Sitting safely in the shelter of Bible discussions among ourselves, or complaining to one another about the horrible state of today's society, does nothing to unleash the power of God. He meets us in the moment of battle. He energizes us when there is an enemy to be pushed back. And the mission of Christ through us is the kingdom of God going forward and pushing back the domain of darkness.[13]

When we live on that edge, when we push the boundaries of darkness and battle on the front lines of faith, we experience Christ profoundly.

In a certain way Christ is closest to us when we pursue His mission fully. And when we are on mission, we find ourselves desperate to pray.

DISTINGUISHED

Giant of the faith Andrew Bonar once said, "God likes to see His people shut up to this, that there is no hope but in prayer. Herein lies the Church's power in the world."

The single feature that distinguishes Christian churches, Christian people, Christian gatherings, and Christian mission is the aroma of prayer. The fact that we pray to the God of the Bible defines us and shapes us as being distinctly and explicitly Christian.

Our connection to and dependence upon prayer is what makes our mission Christ's. Without prayer we run the risk of living a mission that's merely our own. We don't need good ideas, we need God ideas.

The mission of Christ continues in the world today. The goal of the church is to discern what Jesus is already doing and then to join Him. When there's an absence of prayer in our lives, we quickly revert to doing our own thing.

In the absence of prayer our mission ceases to be distinctly Christian.

When we throw our hat into good humanitarian endeavors, ignoring the tool of prayer that changes hearts, situations, and circumstances, we degenerate into secular humanism. We may have good intentions, but they are void of God's power.

We have to pray.

"When we pray as He commanded," wrote Warren Wiersbe, "we will see what He saw, feel what He felt, and do what He did."[14]

The more we pray, the more we gain the heart of God for the world.

And we could use a greater sense of the burden of Jesus *for* people and *against* evil. We need to feel a little bit more of what God feels.

Prayer precipitates joining in the mission of Christ. It realizes that Christian mission is birthed in prayer and continues in prayer.

Prayer is what Christians are called to do.

EXCEEDINGLY MORE

Prayer-soaked, Spirit-filled, gospel-armed mission is always going to be powerful. But it starts with a passion to call upon God and a desire for Him to rend the heavens, come into our circumstances, and show Himself mighty.

Our problem in evangelizing culture is not that we don't have enough preachers or pamphlets. What we lack is a passion for God's presence and power.

One of the most life-shaping sentences for me also came from the book *Fresh Wind, Fresh Fire*, in which Jim Cymbala wrote, "God will manifest Himself in direct proportion to our passion for Him."[15]

To the degree that we are passionate about God—His purposes, His person, and His presence—He will grace us with Himself. But the American church seems to lack this passion, painfully so. We're too easily satisfied.

If we look to history, we see that passion is often birthed amid opposition to Christ's mission. Consider the early church in Acts 4. The people of the church were threatened because they were on mission, and they prayed this way:

> Lord, take note of their threats, and grant that Your bond-servants may speak Your word with all confidence, while You extend Your hand to heal, and signs and wonders take place through the name of Your holy servant Jesus.

The Scripture continues, "And when they had prayed, the place where they had gathered together was shaken, and they were all filled with the Holy Spirit and began to speak the word of God with boldness."[16]

We need to see more displays of the power of Jesus Christ in our churches and in our cities. Not because we are caught up in signs and wonders, but because we are caught up in Jesus, who is powerful!

Can you show me a Jesus who doesn't do these things? He's not in the Bible. Who is this Jesus of the American church who doesn't work miracles?

We need lives that testify not only to the truth of the cross but also to the truth and the power of the empty tomb—the resurrected, wonder-working Son of God. We need to experience the practical power of Christ because He rose and is alive, and He lives in us to reach the world.

Ephesians 3:20 tells us that God is able to do exceedingly beyond anything that we ask, think, or dream, according to the power—the Spirit of Christ—that works in us.

God can do so much more than we even realize!

But we have not because we ask not. In a profound, mysterious, and beautiful way, mission is tied to prayer. What we see in Scripture and across history is that men and women of great faith were always men and women of much prayer.

In Matthew 17, when Jesus came down from the mountain of transfiguration, He met a father whose son was possessed by a demon. The man brought his son to the disciples for healing, but they were unable to help.

The disciples had cast out demons before, but this time they just couldn't do it. They lacked in power, unable to see the mission of Christ go forward in and through them.

Jesus healed the little boy, and later the disciples asked Him, "Why could we not drive it out?"

It was a desperate moment. The disciples failed to help the tormented child. They wanted to understand why they were weak in ministry and why they didn't see more of the power of Christ manifest through them.

Jesus answered their question in Matthew 17:20: "Because of the littleness of your faith; for truly I say to you, if you have faith the size of a mustard seed, you will say to this mountain, 'Move from here to there,' and it will move; and nothing will be impossible for you."[17]

This kind of faith comes through prayer.[18] Christ connects the potency of our faith and the effectiveness of mission to the power of our prayer lives.

"When faith ceases to pray, it ceases to live," said E. M. Bounds.[19] But when fervent prayer yields vibrant faith, momentous obstacles move so that the kingdom of God can go forward.

Think of the obstacles all around us today: the obstacles in our families, for our children, at our workplaces, and in our schools. The obstacles to the gospel, the obstacles to the relief of the poor and oppressed, and the obstacles to the church's effective ministry are enormous.

Yet with vibrant faith, nothing is impossible. The faith that comes by prayer enables the power of Christ to work mightily through us.

BEAN FIELDS

If the church in America and the Christians on TV spent as much time exhorting us to pray as they do asking us for money, we would see transformation in our communities. It's not that we need more funds—we need more prayer. We need the powerful hand of God to move.

I'm an optimist about the church in America and in the world. The more I see Jesus, the more optimistic I am! I believe that the church is ready to pray and enter into a vibrant Spirit-fueled, gospel-armed expression of mission.

Leonard Ravenhill, in his book *Revival Praying*, wrote,

> It is my solemn conviction that the most glorious hour of the Church has yet to be born. All the heroes of faith have not yet been listed. All the chapters of the Church ... have not yet been written. The greatest exploits of faith have yet to be done.[20]

I believe this.

I believe that Jesus wants to do more than we dare to ask or dream. But we have to ask.

"We will only advance in our evangelistic work as fast and as far as we advance on our knees," Alan Redpath warned. He also said,

> Prayer opens the channel between a soul and God; prayerlessness closes it. Prayer releases the grip of Satan's power; prayerlessness increases it. That is why prayer is so exhausting and so vital. If we believed it, the prayer meeting would be as full as the church.[21]

When I think of the need for faithful men and women, I recall a little-known hero of the Old Testament: an Israelite named Shammah.

In 2 Samuel 23, Shammah fought against the Philistines alongside his fellow Israelites. Scripture says, "And the Philistines were gathered into a troop where there was a plot of ground full of lentils."

The Israelites needed to defend the plot of lentils—*a bean field*—but in the face of the enemy, everyone fled. Everyone fled, that is, except for Shammah.

Shammah "took his stand in the midst of the plot, defended it and struck the Philistines," 2 Samuel recounts. "And the LORD brought about a great victory."[22]

Church, where are all the Shammahs today?

Where are the men and women willing to hold ground and defend the inheritance given to us by Christ? Where are the men and women willing to stand firm in the face of opposition and partner with Jesus to work victory on behalf of our families and cities?

Who is going to defend the bean field?

We know that "the weapons of our warfare are not of the flesh, but divinely powerful for the destruction of fortresses."[23] Our plot of ground is our present culture—where Satan sets up camp. Our weapon to defend that ground is prayer.

When the church prays, I believe we can "expect great things from God, and attempt great things for God," as William Carey, the father of modern mission, said.

As you come to the end of this book, my prayer is that you would be moved into mission—and that the first action step you would take is to pray.

Pray that God would burden the church's heart with His burdens.

Pray that He would open our eyes to His mission.

Pray that we would see what He is doing in the world around us and join in.

Pray that He would give us power by His Spirit to be His witnesses.

Pray that God would send us out on mission for His glory.

Church, we are a *sent people*, by the name and power of Jesus, and God created us to live for something bigger than ourselves.

God created us to join Christ's mission to the world.

Now go do it.

BENEDICTION

Brothers and sisters, I pray we would live by the Father's mandate for Missio Christi: that we would be awakened to the mission field around us, take hold of our radical calling, recapture our sense of sent-ness, and go forward into the world in the way of Jesus incarnate.

I pray we would follow the Son's model for Missio Christi: that we would seek people in need of the gospel, that we would touch the outcast and the rejected, that we would free fellow sinners with the grace by which we've been set free, and that we would go forward in mission to see both the oppressed and the oppressor restored.

I pray we would take up the Spirit's ministry through Missio Christi: that by the anointing of the Holy Spirit, we would become agents of renewal in our communities, ushering in the kingdom of God that is both present and future, here and still to come.

Church, I pray that we would know the power and the presence of the risen Christ as we participate in His mission to the world.

Go, that Jesus would be glorified.

Godspeed.

ACKNOWLEDGMENTS

The people who have most impacted my life in pursuing and understanding and enjoying mission are the men, women, and children who are Reality. The local congregations in Santa Barbara, Carpinteria, and Ventura, California, where I pastor and preach, never cease to amaze and inspire me. We discovered and are endeavoring to live these truths together, and I am forever in your debt for continually showing me Jesus. Your examples of life on mission were the inspiration for this book.

The staff and elders at Reality and the Reality church planters have been my theological sounding boards and missional partners. We enjoy Jesus together and help others to do the same, and there is no one else in the world I would rather do that with.

Allison Trowbridge has been my writing partner and has made this project better than I ever could have done alone. Allison, you are amazing, thank you. My agent and dear friend, Don Jacobson, has been and is invaluable to me in writing and life in general. I am deeply grateful to the team at David C Cook for their partnership and vote of confidence. You guys see more possibility than I ever do, and I am blessed to share in this work with you. May God receive much glory from our efforts.

Several friends read through the manuscript of this book and provided helpful feedback, to them I am very thankful. Bryan Norman, thank you for the title and your generous kindness!

Finally, to my love, Kate, and our children, Isaiah and Daisy, thank you for being my best friends and best partners in mission. I love you. Let's always live life at Godspeed together!

NOTES

PREFACE

1. David Kinnaman and Gabe Lyons, *UnChristian: What a New Generation Really Thinks about Christianity … and Why It Matters* (Grand Rapids, MI: Baker, 2007), 34.

CHAPTER 1: MISSION

1. As recorded in J. C. Hoekendijk, "The Church in Missionary Thinking," *International Review of Mission* 41 (1952): 331.
2. John 20:19–21.
3. John Piper, *Let the Nations Be Glad!: The Supremacy of God in Missions*, 3rd ed. (Grand Rapids, MI: Baker Academic, 2010), 15.
4. Exodus 20:3.
5. Mark 12:30.
6. Darrell L. Guder, ed., *Missional Church: A Vision for the Sending of the Church in North America* (Grand Rapids, MI: Eerdmans, 1998), 11.
7. Genesis 12:1–3.
8. Genesis 12:2–3.
9. Deuteronomy 6:4.
10. John 10:30.
11. Matthew 28:19.
12. Norman Geisler, *Systematic Theology*, vol. 2 (Minneapolis, MN: Bethany, 2003) 279.
13. And again in 1 John 4:16.
14. Colossians 1:27.
15. Romans 8:1.
16. John 17:21.
17. David Kinnaman and Gabe Lyons, *UnChristian: What a New Generation Really Thinks about Christianity … and Why It Matters* (Grand Rapids, MI: Baker, 2007), 48.
18. Guder, *Missional Church*, 5.
19. Guder, *Missional Church*, 5.

20. Yvonne Honeycutt, “New Pioneers Leading the Way” in Ralph D. Winter and Steven C. Hawthorne, eds., *Perspectives on the World Christian Movement: A Reader* (Pasadena, CA: William Carey Library, 2009), 377–81.
21. Guder, *Missional Church*, 1.
22. Harvie M. Conn and Manuel Ortiz, *Urban Ministry: The Kingdom, the City & the People of God* (Downers Grove, IL: InterVarsity, 2001), 54.
23. Tom Clegg and Warren Bird, *Lost in America: How You and Your Church Can Impact the World Next Door* (Loveland, CO: Group, 2001), 25; as quoted in “Domestic Missionaries Are Greatly Needed!,” The Navigators, accessed March 13, 2012, www.navigators.org/us/staff/scalabrin/items/Domestic%20Missionaries%20Greatly%20Needed!
24. Guder, *Missional Church*, 4.

CHAPTER 2: CALL

1. Mark 1:16–20.
2. Mark 1:14–15.
3. John 1.
4. John 2:1.
5. John 2:13–25.
6. John 3:22–24.
7. 1 Peter 2:9; see also 1 Peter 4:10.
8. 1 Corinthians 3:9; 2 Corinthians 6:1.
9. Exodus 33:5; Isaiah 30:1; Ezekiel 3:7.
10. 1 Corinthians 1:26–29.
11. 1 Corinthians 1:27.
12. Matthew 14:15.
13. Matthew 19:13.
14. Luke 9:54.
15. Matthew 26:40, 45. See also John MacArthur, *The MacArthur New Testament Commentary: Matthew 1–7* (Chicago: Moody, 1985), 117.
16. MacArthur, *The MacArthur New Testament Commentary: Matthew 1–7*, 117.
17. Mark 1:17.
18. Ephesians 5:1; Romans 8:29.

19. R. T. France, *The New International Greek Testament Commentary: The Gospel of Mark* (Grand Rapids, MI: Eerdmans, 2002), 96.
20. John 15:16.
21. Luke 14:25–35.
22. Mark 10:28.
23. Luke 5:5.
24. Kenneth E. Bailey, *Jesus Through Middle Eastern Eyes: Cultural Studies in the Gospels* (Downers Grove, IL: InterVarsity, 2008), 146.
25. See Luke 5:8–11.
26. See Luke 15.
27. "The Harvest Is Plentiful," Missio Christi, accessed February 23, 2012, http://missiochristi.net/your-story/post/962931?lastPage=true.
28. Matthew 9:36–37.
29. Mark 3:13–14.
30. Acts 4:7.
31. Luke 5:8.
32. Isaiah 6:5.
33. James 4:6.

CHAPTER 3: SENT

1. David Kinnaman and Gabe Lyons, *UnChristian: What a New Generation Really Thinks about Christianity … and Why It Matters* (Grand Rapids, MI: Baker, 2007), 34.
2. Andreas J. Köstenberger, Peter T. O'Brien, and D. A. Carson, eds., *Salvation to the Ends of the Earth: A Biblical Theology of Mission* (Downers Grove, IL: InterVarsity, 2001), 208.
3. Hebrews 1:1–2 NLT.
4. John 7:29.
5. Köstenberger, O'Brien, Carson, *Salvation to the Ends of the Earth*, 209. See also John 7:29; 15:21; 17:8, 25.
6. Kinnaman and Lyons, *UnChristian*, 48.
7. John 17:26.
8. Stephen Seamands, *Ministry in the Image of God: The Trinitarian Shape of Christian Service* (Downers Grove, IL: IVP, 2005), 161.

9. Ephesians 4:15.
10. *Merriam-Webster's Collegiate Dictionary*, Eleventh Edition, s.v. "judge."
11. Romans 13:1–4.
12. Ephesians 6:10–24.
13. Matthew 7:3–4.
14. See Luke 6:35.
15. Matthew 5:44–45; Luke 6:35.
16. Luke 23:34.
17. Miroslav Volf, *Free of Charge: Giving and Forgiving in a Culture Stripped of Grace* (Grand Rapids, MI: Zondervan, 2005), 141.
18. Romans 12:19.
19. Romans 12:17–19.
20. Martin Luther, *LW*, 31:306, as quoted in Volf, *Free of Charge*, 199.
21. Matthew 6:12.

CHAPTER 4: INCARNATION

1. Dick Staub, *The Culturally Savvy Christian: A Manifesto for Deepening Faith and Enriching Popular Culture in an Age of Christianity-Lite* (San Francisco: Jossey-Bass, 2007), 29–36.
2. John 17:15.
3. Ephesians 6:12.
4. David Kinnaman and Gabe Lyons, *UnChristian: What a New Generation Really Thinks about Christianity … and Why It Matters* (Grand Rapids, MI: Baker, 2007), 26.
5. Kinnaman and Lyons, *UnChristian*, 27.
6. John 17:15.
7. Kinnaman and Lyons, *UnChristian*, 27.
8. John 17:16, 18.
9. 1 Peter 2:5, 9.
10. John Stott, *The Living Church: Convictions of a Lifelong Pastor* (Downers Grove, IL: InterVarsity, 2007), 54–55.
11. Stott, *Living Church*, 20.
12. Jeremiah 31:3; Hosea 11:4; Romans 2:4.

13. Jerry Cook, *Love, Acceptance, and Forgiveness: Being Christian in a Non-Christian World* (Ventura, CA: Regal, 2009), 81.
14. In his classic book *Love, Acceptance, and Forgiveness*, Jerry Cook referred to this as the "Immanuel Principle." See page 81 of the second edition (2009).
15. Dallas Willard, "Is Poverty Spiritual?" in *The Spirit of the Disciplines: Understanding How God Changes Lives* (New York: HarperCollins, 1991).
16. John Corrie, ed., *Dictionary of Mission Theology* (Downers Grove, IL: IVP Academic, 2007), 177.
17. Matthew 10:29.
18. Michael Frost, *Exiles: Living Missionally in a Post-Christian Culture* (Peabody, MA: Hendrickson, 2006), 54.
19. Os Hillman, International Coalition of Workplace Ministries, "Faith & Work Factsheet," Marketplace Leaders, accessed February 6, 2012, www.marketplaceleaders.org/faith-work-factsheet/.
20. Dallas Willard, *Spirit of the Disciplines*, 214.
21. Brian Pederson, posted on http://missiochristi.net/, November 12, 2009.
22. Gideon, posted on http://missiochristi.net/, November 13, 2009.
23. Romans 1:16.
24. Frost, *Exiles*, 55.
25. On the Missio Christi website, we posted a message I did on truth in the postmodern era. The message focuses on the presuppositions, assumptions, and results of the premodern era and the modern era (which ended a few decades ago) along with the postmodern mind-set that pervades our culture today.
26. George R. Hunsberger and Craig Van Gelder, eds., *The Church Between Gospel and Culture: The Emerging Mission in North America* (Grand Rapids, MI: Eerdmans, 1996), 258.
27. Kinnaman and Lyons, *UnChristian*, 29.
28. Kinnaman and Lyons, *UnChristian*, 27.
29. Barna Research, as cited in Staub, *Culturally Savvy Christian*, 25.
30. Matthew 5:16.
31. Ephesians 4:15.
32. George Gallup Jr. and Timothy Jones, *The Next American Spirituality: Finding God in the Twenty-First Century* (Colorado Springs, CO: David C Cook, 2000), 45.

33. Lesslie Newbigin, *The Gospel in a Pluralist Society* (Grand Rapids, MI: Eerdmans, 1989), 135.

CHAPTER 5: SEEK

1. See John 4.
2. John 4:4 KJV.
3. Luke 9:51–56.
4. John 4:27.
5. Genesis 24:11; 29:7–8.
6. Genesis 24:11; Exodus 2:16; 1 Samuel 9:11.
7. Andreas J. Köstenberger, *Baker Exegetical Commentary on the New Testament: John* (Grand Rapids, MI: Baker Academic, 2004), 151.
8. See Luke 5:1–3.
9. 2 Corinthians 4:6–8.
10. Daniel T. Niles, *This Jesus … Whereof We Are Witnesses* (Philadelphia: Westminster, 1965), 23–27.
11. Niles, *This Jesus*, 23–27.
12. Philippians 2:7–8 NLT.
13. See Mark 6:7–13.
14. David Kinnaman and Gabe Lyons, *UnChristian: What a New Generation Really Thinks about Christianity … and Why It Matters* (Grand Rapids, MI: Baker, 2007), 31.
15. Kinnaman and Lyons, *UnChristian*, 68.
16. John 1:18.
17. 2 Corinthians 5:14.
18. John 4:28–42.

CHAPTER 6: TOUCH

1. Mark 1:39–42.
2. Paul Brand, as quoted in R. Kent Hughes, *Mark Volume One: Jesus, Servant and Savior* (Westchester, IL: Crossway, 1989), 54.
3. Hughes, *Mark Volume One*, 58.
4. Luke 5:12.
5. Leviticus 13:45–46.

6. *Merriam-Webster's Collegiate Dictionary*, Eleventh Edition, s.v. "stigma."
7. Hughes, *Mark Volume One*, 55.
8. Luke 17:12.
9. William Barclay, *The Gospel of Matthew, Volume Two* (Philadelphia: Westminster, 1958), 301.
10. Robert A. Guelich, *Word Biblical Commentary*, vol. 34a (Nashville, TN: Thomas Nelson, 1989), 74.
11. Matthew 10:8.
12. See 1 Corinthians 6:7–11.
13. Matthew 11:5; Luke 7:22.
14. Matthew 8:1.
15. R. T. France, *The New International Greek Testament Commentary: The Gospel of Mark* (Grand Rapids, MI: Eerdmans, 2002), 116–17.
16. Matthew 9:36; 14:14; 15:32; 20:34; Mark 6:34; 8:2; Luke 7:13.
17. Isaiah 53:4.
18. As told in John Stott, *The Incomparable Christ* (Downers Grove, IL: InterVarsity, 2001), 143.
19. Matthew 11:5; Luke 7:22.
20. Mark 1:39.
21. Matthew 25:40, 45.
22. Proverbs 19:17.
23. Mary Kugler, "Leprosy (Hansen's Disease)," About.com Rare Diseases, accessed February 6, 2012, http://rarediseases.about.com/cs/infectiousdisease/a/071203.htm.
24. Galatians 6:10.
25. Hebrews 13:16.

CHAPTER 7: FREE

1. See John 8:1–11.
2. Romans 6:23.
3. David Kinnaman and Gabe Lyons, *UnChristian: What a New Generation Really Thinks about Christianity … and Why It Matters* (Grand Rapids, MI: Baker, 2007), 34.
4. See Jonah 3:10–4:11.
5. John 8:4.

6. Leviticus and Deuteronomy.
7. John 8:7.
8. Luke 4:20.
9. Luke 4:21.
10. Romans 2:4.
11. See John 8:11.
12. Read more at www.graceisforsinners.com/interview/#ixzz19xcgFEbF. Under Creative Commons License: Attribution Non-Commercial No Derivatives.
13. John 8:7.
14. Read more at www.graceisforsinners.com/tag/personal/. Under Creative Commons License: Attribution Non-Commercial No Derivatives.
15. Colossians 2:14.

CHAPTER 8: RESTORE

1. Matthew 25:40 NLT.
2. Luke 19:1–9.
3. Matthew 5:1–12.
4. Luke 18:35–43.
5. Kenneth E. Bailey, *Jesus Through Middle Eastern Eyes: Cultural Studies in the Gospels* (Downers Grove, IL: InterVarsity, 2008), 179–80.
6. "U.S. charitable giving estimated to be $307.65 billion in 2008," Giving USA Foundation, accessed February 7, 2012, www.philanthropy.iupui.edu/News/2009/docs/GivingReaches300billion_06102009.pdf.
7. Arthur C. Brooks, "A Nation of Givers," *The American*, March/April 2008, www.american.com/archive/2008/march-april-magazine-contents/a-nation-of-givers.
8. "Quick Facts About Nonprofits," National Center for Charitable Statistics, accessed February 7, 2012, http://nccs.urban.org/statistics/quickfacts.cfm.
9. Mark 2:17 NLT.
10. Bailey, *Jesus Through Middle Eastern Eyes*, 180.
11. Brennan Manning, *The Furious Longing of God* (Colorado Springs, CO: David C Cook, 2009), 84–85.
12. John Dickson, *Promoting the Gospel: A Practical Guide to the Biblical Art of Sharing Your Faith* (Sydney, Australia: Blue Bottle, 2005), 41.

13. Luke 6:20, 24; 8:14; 12:15–34; 14:33; 16:13–14; 18:18–30.

14. Luke 16:13 NLT.

15. Timothy Keller, *Counterfeit Gods: The Empty Promises of Money, Sex, and Power, and the Only Hope that Matters* (New York: Dutton, 2009), 63.

16. Luke 19:9.

17. Romans 2:4.

CHAPTER 9: RENEW

1. See Mark 5:1–20.

2. Numbers 19:11–14.

3. Leviticus 11:7; Deuteronomy 14:8.

4. Acts 1:4–8.

5. Acts 2:14–41.

6. Acts 10:19.

7. Acts 13:1–2.

8. Acts 16:6–10.

9. Romans 8:14.

10. Galatians 5:16.

11. Ephesians 5:18.

12. Revelation 2:7.

13. Galatians 2:20.

14. Alexander Pope, "An Essay on Criticism" (1709).

15. Acts 1:8.

16. David Kinnaman and Gabe Lyons, *UnChristian: What a New Generation Really Thinks about Christianity … and Why It Matters* (Grand Rapids, MI: Baker, 2007), 48.

17. Kinnaman and Lyons, *UnChristian*, 47.

18. Kinnaman and Lyons, *UnChristian*, 49–50.

19. Kinnaman and Lyons, *UnChristian*, 23.

20. Ralph Vartabedian and Ken Bensinger, "Toyota's gas-pedal problems grow," *Los Angeles Times*, January 28, 2010, http://articles.latimes.com/2010/jan/28/business/la-fi-toyota-stop28-2010jan28.

21. See Mark 6:53–56; 7:31–32.

22. Compare with John 15:11.

CHAPTER 10: KINGDOM

1. "Walking in Obedience," Missio Christi, accessed February 8, 2012, http://missiochristi.net/your-story/post/942683.
2. Mark 1:9–17.
3. Luke 19:38.
4. Matthew 21:5.
5. Revelation 19:16.
6. Philippians 2:11.
7. Matthew 4:16.
8. John 12:31; Ephesians 2:2; 1 John 5:19.
9. John 10:10.
10. 2 Timothy 2:26; Hebrews 2:15.
11. John 12, Ephesians 2, 1 John 5.
12. John 12:31; 16:11; Hebrews 2:14–15; 1 John 3:8.
13. John 1:9.
14. John 8:36.
15. Matthew 4:17.
16. Ephesians 2:1–3; Hebrews 6:1.
17. Matthew 6:24; Luke 16:13.
18. Ephesians 2:1–9.
19. John 3:3 NLT.
20. Matthew 9:21–22; Luke 8:36.
21. Matthew 8:16–17.
22. 1 Peter 2:24.
23. Acts 12:5; 2 Timothy 2:26.
24. Luke 18:35–43.
25. 2 Corinthians 4:4.
26. Mark 1:38.
27. "Iran: Maryam and Marzieh Free," The Voice of the Martyrs, accessed February 8, 2012, www.persecution.com/public/newsroom.aspx?story_ID=MjA0.
28. Kurt Badenhausen, "America's Most Miserable Cities," *Forbes*, www.forbes.com/2009/02/06/most-miserable-cities-business-washington_0206_miserable_cities.html.

29. Matthew 19:30; 20:16; Mark 10:31; Luke 13:30.

30. Luke 22:24–27; Matthew 5:5; 18:4.

31. "A Luke 14 Thanksgiving," Missio Christi, accessed February 8, 2012, http://missiochristi.net/your-story/post/954448.

32. Luke 14:16–24.

33. 1 Corinthians 10:33.

34. John 8:34, 36.

35. Matthew 12:28.

36. Luke 10:17.

37. Luke 10:8–9.

38. 1 Corinthians 13:13 NLT.

39. Philippians 3:10.

40. Revelation 21:4.

41. Matthew 16:24.

42. Matthew 16:25.

43. 2 Corinthians 11:24–28.

44. Acts 14:22.

45. Matthew 24:13; 2 Thessalonians 3:13; Hebrews 10:26; 12:1–2; James 1:12; Revelation 14:12.

46. 2 Timothy 2:12.

47. See 2 Corinthians 12:9.

CHAPTER 11: PRAY

1. Luke 11:1.

2. Mark 1:35.

3. Matthew 14:23.

4. Luke 6:12.

5. Revelation 5:8.

6. James 4:2.

7. See Exodus 32:7–14.

8. Ezekiel 22:30–31.

9. 1 John 5:14.

10. Matthew 28:19–20.

11. Hudson Taylor, as quoted in J. Oswald Sanders, *Christ Indwelling and Enthroned: 14 Inspiring Messages to Help You Walk in Victory* (Santa Ana, CA: Calvary Chapel, 2002), 61.

12. Charles Haddon Spurgeon, "A Call to Worship" sermon (1873), as quoted in Jim Cymbala, *Fresh Wind, Fresh Fire: What Happens When God's Spirit Invades the Hearts of His People* (Grand Rapids, MI: Zondervan, 1997), 25.

13. Cymbala, *Fresh Wind*, 200–1.

14. Warren W. Wiersbe, *Be Loyal: Following the King of Kings*, 2nd edition (Colorado Springs, CO: David C Cook, 2008), 83.

15. Cymbala, *Fresh Wind*, 153.

16. Acts 4:29–31.

17. Matthew 17:14–20.

18. Matthew 17:21; Mark 9:29.

19. E. M. Bounds, as quoted in Leonard Ravenhill, *Revival Praying: An Urgent and Powerful Message for the Family of Christ* (Bloomington, MN: Bethany, 2005), 33.

20. Ravenhill, *Revival Praying*, 33.

21. "Inspirational Quotes," HistoryMakers, accessed February 8, 2012, www.historymakers.info/stuff/resources.html.

22. 2 Samuel 23:11–12.

23. 2 Corinthians 10:4.